Sigurd F. Olson

is known by a generation of wilderness canoemen as the Bourgeois, as *voyageurs* of old
called their trusted leaders. The author of
*The Singing Wilderness, Listening Point, The
Lonely Land*, and *Runes of the North* is one
of our country's well-known woodsmen and
naturalists. Born in Chicago in 1899, educated
at the University of Wisconsin (Geology)
and the University of Illinois (Plant and Animal Ecology), he was a professor and dean
until he began devoting himself entirely to
wilderness interpretation and its preservation.
Mr. Olson is a former President of the National Parks Association, and is still a member of its Board of Trustees. He serves on the
Council of the Wilderness Society and as a
consultant to the Izaak Walton League of
America, the President's Quetico-Superior
Committee, and since 1962 the Department of
the Interior. His home is in Ely, Minnesota,
gateway to the canoe country.

Other Books by Sigurd F. Olson

THE LONELY LAND (1961)

LISTENING POINT (1958)

THE SINGING WILDERNESS (1956)

These are Borzoi Books
published by ALFRED A. KNOPF *in New York*

RUNES OF THE NORTH

Sigurd F. Olson

RUNES OF

New York

Illustrations by Robert Hines

THE NORTH

Alfred A. Knopf   1964

L. C. catalog card number: 63–18356

THIS IS A BORZOI BOOK,
PUBLISHED BY ALFRED A. KNOPF, INC.

PUBLISHED SEPTEMBER 16, 1963
REPRINTED TWICE
FOURTH PRINTING, MARCH 1964

The following chapters have appeared in somewhat different form: "Hunting Moon" in *Country Beautiful*, "Wild Rice" in *Gourmet*, and "Alaskan Wilderness" as "Runes of the Far North" in *American Forests*.

To Elizabeth

ACKNOWLEDGMENTS

I AM DEEPLY GRATEFUL FOR criticism, editing, and help, to members of my family, my agent Marie Rodell, and my editor Angus Cameron. Sincere appreciation goes to Ann Langen for her patient and enthusiastic work during the entire preparation of the manuscript. I also wish to thank my good friend Harlan Lampe for calling my attention to *Kalevala;* Eric Morse, historian and fellow *voyageur*, for geographical checking of routes; and Gerry Malaher, Chief of the Game Division of Manitoba, for his assistance on the caribou study.

I am indebted to the following: Aili Kolehmainen Johnson and The Book Concern for permission to use excerpts from the Finnish epic poem *Kalevala;* Loren Eiseley and Random

House for quotations from *The Immense Journey;* Anya Seton and Houghton Mifflin Company for an episode from *The Winthrop Woman;* Phebe Jewell Nichols for the "Menominee Cradle Song" in her book *Tales from an Indian Lodge;* Fred Morgan and *The Beaver* magazine of the Hudson's Bay Company for information in the article "Wild Rice Harvest" (autumn 1960); Walter O'Meara and Bobbs-Merrill Company for the statement on Daniel Harmon in the book *The Grand Portage;* The Champlain Society of Canada for use of material from *David Thompson's Narrative of Explorations in Western America 1784-1812,* edited by J. B. Tyrrell; Robert Service and Dodd, Mead and Company for several quotations from *The Collected Poems of Robert Service; True* Magazine for an adaptation of my story "Trout of the Outlaw Country"; and *The Naturalist.*

Among many sources that supplied valuable information are: *The Journals of Alexander Henry the Younger and David Thompson, 1799-1814* (New York: Francis P. Harper; 1897); Alexander Henry: *Travels and Adventures in Canada and the Indian Territories between the years 1760 and 1776,* edited by James Baine (Little Brown and Co.); *The Fur Trade of Canada* by Harold Innis (New Haven: Yale University Press; 1930); *Five Fur Traders of the Northwest,* edited by Charles M. Gates (Minneapolis, Minn.: University of Minnesota Press; 1933); *Son of the North* by Charles Camsell (Toronto: Ryerson Press; 1954); *Peter Pond Fur Trader and Adventurer* by H. A. Innis (Toronto: Irwin and Gordon Ltd.; 1930); *The*

ACKNOWLEDGMENTS

Moose Fort Journals, published by the Hudson's Bay Record Society of London; *Bogs of the Quetico-Superior* by J. E. Potzger, Department of Botany, Butler University, Indiana; Bulletin 102 of the Bureau of American Ethnology, Washington, D. C.; *The Caribou Crisis* by A. W. F. Banfield, Canadian Wildlife Service, as reprinted from *The Beaver* 1956.

My thanks for many courtesies and help goes to members of the Hudson's Bay Company all over the north; to Jock McNiven, Superintendent of Eldorado Mine on Great Bear Lake, Angus Sherwood of Norman Wells on the Mackenzie, Barney Lamm of Kenora and Ralph Hedlin of Winnipeg for the flight to Nejanilini, Joe Langevin of the Kluane Game Sanctuary in the Yukon; to Urban C. Nelson, U. S. Fish and Wildlife Service, Leone J. Mitchel of Glacier Bay National Monument, Samuel A. King of Mt. McKinley National Park, James W. Brooks of the Alaska Department of Fish and Game, Jess Honeywell of the Bureau of Land Management, and P. D. Hanson of the U. S. Forest Service, and their staffs, all of Alaska; and to many others who over the years have helped and given of their time and enthusiastic support wherever I have gone.

CONTENTS

CONTENTS

PART II: PAYS D'EN HAUT

PROEM

Only I am left to sing these tales learned from riddles, snatched from the wayside, broken from the heather, torn from the bushes, drawn from the waters, rubbed from the blades of grass, and reft from the roadside. ********

The frost squeaked out verses to me, and the rain chanted runes. The winds whistled other lays carried by the waves of the sea. Birds twittered words, and the boughs of the trees whispered charms.

These I twined into a ball which was carried in my sledge to a barn where the grain dried. The ball of verse was placed into a copper casket, hidden on a beam of the barn loft.

My verses waited in the cold; long they yearned in the darkness. *** Shall I draw forth my songs from the chilly frost? **** Shall I open the chest of words, set tune to phrases, unwind the ball, and straighten out the knots in the yarns?

—*Kalevala*

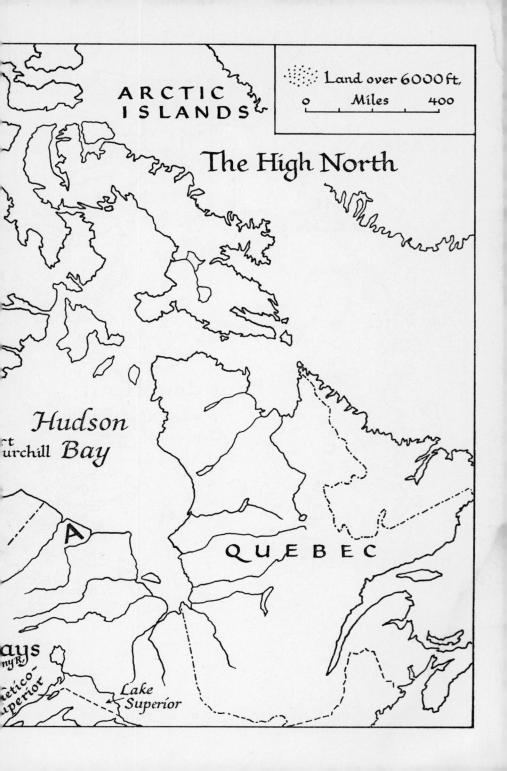

ARCTIC
ISLANDS

Land over 6000 ft.

0   Miles   400

The High North

Hudson
urchill Bay
rt

A

QUEBEC

ays
ny R.
nético-
uperior

Lake
Superior

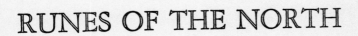

RUNES OF THE NORTH

RUNES OF THE NORTH

L IKE THE ancient bard in the Finnish epic poem *Kalevala*, I have listened to the rapids of rivers, to the winds of summer and winter, and to the waves of many lakes. I have known mountains and glaciers, forests and tundras, and have gathered runes wherever I have gone. Only a few are part of the legendry of the past; most have to do with what I have known and done, thoughts and impressions which have come to me in my home country of the Quetico-Superior, in the far Canadian north, and in Alaska.

My runes have come from the wilderness, for in its solitude, silence, and freedom, I see more clearly those values and influences that over the long centuries have molded us as a race. I know there are moments of insight when ancient truths do stand out more vividly, and one senses anew his relationship to the earth and to all life. Such moments are worth waiting for, and when they come in some unheralded instant of knowing, they are of the purest gold.

"Man," as Emerson once said, "is a dwarf of himself and so ancient beliefs and feelings are in a sense vestigial remains of the common origins of man's inner world."

This inner world has to do with the wilderness from which we came, timelessness, cosmic rhythms, and the deep feelings men have for an unchanged environment. It is a oneness and communion with nature, a basic awareness of beauty, and earth wisdom which since the beginning of man's rise from the primitive have nourished his visions and dreams.

Many have gathered runes and searched for meanings, with understanding hearts and open minds. Such meanings can never be measured, for they belong to the shadowy realm of the intangibles. They are more real and significant, perhaps, than what can be seen, for they have given rise to all the achievements of the spirit and to all cultural advance.

If my runes may have touched something of man's ancient dream, revealed some of the common origins of his long past, and restored some sense of balance, wholeness, and perspective, then my gatherings will have been worthwhile. Should the reader catch even a glimmering of the almost forgotten joys of simplicity, contentment, and fullness that are found in the wilderness, that is enough.

LE BEAU PAYS

LE BEAU PAYS

The Beautiful Land

THIS IS HOW *early* voyageurs and explorers spoke of the land of the Rainy River long ago. After traversing the Quetico-Superior country, a series of rugged picturesque lakes connected by rapids, falls, and many portages, they finally left the island-dotted expanses of Lac la Pluie and drifted down a broad and quiet river flowing serenely through an almost pastoral region of meadows and gentle terrain toward the broad waters of Lake of the Woods. It was such a contrast to what they had known, reminded them so much of the tranquil rivers of Europe, that they always thought of it as "Le Beau Pays."

But to modern voyageurs, the land they crossed to reach it is the true "Le Beau Pays," and to many there is no finer canoe country on the continent. The intricate labyrinth of waterways and forests lying for over two hundred miles along the Minnesota-Ontario border between Grand Portage Post on

7

the northwest coast of Lake Superior and the Rainy River seems made for enjoyment and wilderness travel.

It is the ancient land of the Chippewas. Moose and deer are found there, and beaver still build their dams along its streams. The hermit thrush, the white-throat, and the loon are heard at dusk and in the spring the partridges drum. Here are stands of tall red and white pine, redolent cedars, silvery birch, and golden fields of rice.

Its campsites, clean and close to the water's edge, are paved with smooth glaciated granite, for this is the southern rim of the Canadian Shield. Even the air seems rarefied and, in early morning, there is a high mountain freshness and sparkle that makes one think of timberline. Here there is intimacy, vistas of rare poetic beauty—and everywhere is delight. To me it is home, a land to remember and return to.

CHAPTER I

THE DREAM NET

A CHIPPEWA WOMAN gave the dream net to me when I left Grand Portage Indian Reservation on Lake Superior. It was an unusual gift and it pleased me, for Indians do not give their charms lightly to strangers. I examined the little net of fine thread strung tightly on its four-inch hoop of ash, turned it over and over in my hands wondering wherein its secret lay. It was shaped like a perfect spider's web with a hole in the very center.

9

She asked me to take it home and hang it over the beds of my children, said it meant good luck and pleasant dreams. When she saw the question in my eyes, she explained how bad dreams as well as good were always in the air around sleeping children, that the bad ones waited for dusk and if there were nothing to stop them a child might scream.

I listened, delighted with the idea, and thought of the times I had awakened in terror as a child, and of the many times my own boys had whimpered and moaned in their sleep.

The Indian woman continued and told me how in the days long before the white man came, a dream net hung in every tepee in the village because mothers wanted their babies to go into the dream world in peace and awaken with quiet eyes.

The net was beautifully made, with the center opening not more than a quarter of an inch in size. I held it out to her and asked the reason for the hole.

She smiled tolerantly and explained it was where the good dreams came through the net; the bad ones, not knowing how, were tangled in the mesh and when the light struck them in the morning, they died.

I tucked the dream net gently into my pack, tried to show my faith and was rewarded by a smile. That night when I returned, I told my two little boys the legend of the Chippewa and hung the net between their beds. There it stayed for years until the boys grew up and went away. Though they are now far past the age when they can be expected to believe such delightful fantasies, I am sure they have not entirely forgotten and sometimes, when they close their eyes at night, they still may sleep with the calm assurance that their dreams are guarded well. Their years of childhood faith, I believe, left a mark upon them and as proof, the little net was eventually hung over another little bed in far-off Alaska. The net accomplished its purpose as it had for the Chippewa over centuries of time.

What the Indian woman told me spoke of love and tenderness toward children, a trait of character I found in the north and among all Indian tribes wherever I have been. But it was with the Menominees of Wisconsin that I found an interpretation of an ancient cradle song which to me embodies all of the beauty and poetry of the legend itself.

Ne pa Ko my sleepy head,
In your basswood cradle bed
Downy cushioned gently swaying
To the song the winds are playing,
Homeward whippoorwills are winging
Hear them now their sleep song singing—
Sleep, little warrior, sleep.

Ne pa Ko my sleepy head,
The golden bees have gone to bed,
Silver, grey-green dragon flies
Close their luminous great eyes,
Wings of silken moths are still,

Pine birds call you from the hill—
Sleep, little warrior, sleep.

Ne pa Ko, my sleepy head,
Tiger lily's gone to bed
Where the heron tall and stately
Watches for the moon sedately,
In the swamp the marsh hen drowses
Near the muskrat's winter houses—
Sleep, little warrior, sleep.

Winds are whispering in the balsams,
Singing softly in the cedars,
Crooning through the glistening birches—
Sleep, little warrior, sleep.

In the dream net that Indian mother gave me long ago, I hear this song. Good dreams are there, dreams of birds and butterflies, and the wind over the marshes. When I lie in my sleeping bag and listen to the soft moaning of the pines, the lap of the waves, or sounds of night birds in the trees, I often think of it. Sleep comes swiftly then, for there is a dream net over me wherever I may be. I have thought of it in many places, when bedded down on the tundras of the far north, in the mountains of the west, the lowlands of the south, or the highlands of the east. I have seen it in interlacing branches overhead, in hovering cliffs and in the snow-clad peaks of mountain ranges, even in the stars themselves. When I happen to remember, the net is always there, whether I am sleeping under a tree, against a log, or in some leafy hollow next to a ledge. On nights when the roar of some rapids we must run in the morning might have kept me from sleep, it has been a comfort.

We smile tolerantly at such beliefs but cannot ignore them, for in all peoples, no matter what the race, there is always an intuitive sense of a spirit world. To the Indians of earlier days, this spirit world was very real. To them all living things have spirits and one must recognize that they exist and that people must live with them or die. Before any creature is killed, its spirit must be spoken to; before a plant is taken for use, it must be approached with reverence and explanations. When an Indian mother makes medicine for her children, she invokes her own guardian spirit to guide her to the proper plant and for skill in compounding a cure. When she finds what she has been searching for, she invokes the spirit of the plant itself and takes it with gratitude and faith. If death results, it merely means that the great Manitou has called the loved one to the Happy Hunting Grounds for reasons of his own.

Such implicit faith can never be explained through reason or cold scientific analysis. Back of it are a million years of racial experience when men lived as did other creatures, with only one purpose, physical survival: finding enough food, shelter from the elements, and producing young to perpetuate the species. Yet, back somewhere in those dark and misty regions of the past, some mind must have broken from the old pattern of brutishness and showed the first vague intimations of something different, its evidence perhaps nothing more than a gesture of affection or an impulse to share a morsel of food with the dead. Whatever it was, or however it came about, here was a dividing line between primitiveness and a new world of imagination and spiritual awareness, the great leap in the evolution of the race. Granted that creatures other than man show love and feeling not only for their young but for each other, only in man has it progressed to where it is a major force in his development and culture.

All this is a legacy from the dusk where magic once ruled. It is part of the inheritance of longings, hopes, and fears that came to men when they gazed into their fires at night, into the blue distances, or at the stars, and dreamed strange dreams of beauty and peopled the unknown with many forms. Though this was during the childhood of the human race, the wonder and the dreams live on and play a role in all our lives. Here is the creative force in art, music, literature, and religion, the wellspring from which all our progress comes.

Many dreams are those of beauty and, like the Navajo, those close to the earth and not too far removed from the ancient spirit world, can pray with them and say:

Beauty is before me.
Beauty is behind me.
Beauty is below me.

THE DREAM NET

Beauty is above me.
I walk in beauty.

My little dream net spoke of many things to me, of love for children, of tolerance and the intangible qualities which give warmth and meaning to life. When I accepted it, I did so with humility because for me it was a symbol not only of trust and acceptance by my Indian friend, but a hint of the long past and a world of dreams most moderns have forgotten.

Not long ago I slept under a pine tree with my six-year-old grandson Derek. We had had a tiny fire and lay in our sleeping bags watching the reflection of dying embers against the branches and how it turned them to gold and bronze and copper. I told him many stories of moose and bear and, at the end, the legend of the dream net; he believed, for he was young and still had faith. Above us that night was the ancient net, and the night was full of dreams both good and bad. He could see them, feel them, and when I told him that only the good ones came through, he closed his eyes quietly and went to sleep.

Later when the fire had died and the stars were bright, as they are when one looks up at them through tall dark pines, I wakened him and we lay watching together. His eyes were big and full of wonder as I pointed out the Great Bear, Cassiopeia, and the Pleiades, and the vast expanse of the Milky Way. Once we saw a falling star. It streaked across the heavens from east to west, a glittering cascade of shattered light.

15

"Papa," he said excitedly, "why did that star fall?"

I tried to explain but his young mind was not ready for talk of disintegrating matter, oxidation, burning in the stratosphere, and the bombardment of the earth with intersteller dust and meteorites. So I simply said:

"Stars fall like the leaves of trees; sometimes they get tired of holding on away up there and just let go, and then they fall."

My explanation satisfied him completely. There was nothing more to say.

"Do you suppose we might find one someday?" he asked finally. And I told him if we looked real hard, we might find one lying in the woods in the morning, and with that his eyes closed again and he was asleep.

I could not help but think as we lay there of what Loren Eiseley said: "Men troubled at last by the things they build, may toss in their sleep and dream bad dreams, or lie awake while the meteors whisper greenly overhead, but nowhere in all space or on a thousand worlds will there be men to share our loneliness."

All this Derek could not understand and it was just as well, but he knew beauty and wonder as he watched the falling star. To him it was only a dream, but nevertheless one with the dreams and hopes of all mankind.

Another night I lay on a lonely point of rock in the Quetico-Superior country. Again the stars were bright and I watched for the meteors I knew would come that season of the year.

For a long time there was nothing, only the vast swirling nebulae, then across the heavens went a streak of light. I did not hear it whisper, nor was it green. It flamed for a moment like a torch of sparkling fire and then disappeared. I thought again of Eiseley's words and the consciousness of man's scientific achievements came home to me; the universe now of a size beyond imagining, the earth floating like a grain of dust in the void. Here I lay on a rock, a tiny living speck of sensitive protoplasm and, for a moment, I felt lost and alone with what I knew.

Lying there, the story of the dream net did not seem to matter, nor did any of the other legends, traditions, or beliefs of men in the spirit world. Protons, neutrons, neutrinos, space time, these were the real things—and thinking of what they meant I was troubled.

But then I remembered a night on a glaciological survey with the famous geologist Dr. Wallace Atwood. We had found an island with a beautiful outcrop of Saganaga porphyry, something he had wanted to see for a long time. Porphyry had a special meaning for him and he had looked for rare specimens of the rock all over the world.

We sat before our fire that night and talked about the glacial patterns we had seen over the Canadian Shield, but mostly we spoke about porphyry and when he fondled the prize specimen in his hand, his eyes shone with delight.

"Tell me, Dr. Atwood," I said finally, "how is it that at the age of eighty-four, you still get as much pleasure and excitement out of a find like this as though you were a student on your first expedition?"

He looked at the bit of porphyry again, turned it so the light gleamed on its surfaces. It was a perfect piece and I knew it would go back with him when the survey was completed.

"The secret," he said, "is never to lose the power of wonder at the mystery of the universe. If you keep that, you stay young forever. If you lose it, you die."

The power of wonder, imagination—the sense of mystery and belief—that is what I saw in Derek's eyes that night under the pine tree. The same light and faith were in the eyes of the Indian woman of Grand Portage when she said: "The bad dreams get caught in the net, the good ones come through."

I forgot my ponderings and settled down in my bag. Though the simple legend of the dream net was only an infinitesimal bit of the whole fabric of the dream world, a fabric that has brought beauty and meaning to searching minds for untold generations, it was in its way perhaps as important as any other.

Myriads of stars were my net that night, but I no longer felt lonely, for I knew that while man might unravel the puzzled skein of life and solve the riddles of the universe, what really matters is the wonder which makes it all possible. Back of everything is always a net of dreams.

CHAPTER 2

THE EXPLORERS

THERE IS MAGIC in venturing into the unknown for the first time, especially when one is young. While the magic is never wholly lost in later life, it is when life is all romance and poetry that it can be known to its fullest. Each generation going into the lake country of the Quetico-Superior discovers this for itself and the impact is never forgotten. Though my first expedition was forty years ago, the impressions that were mine seem as vivid today as they were then.

Often it comes back to me, the day when with three companions I paddled away from the little logging town of Win-

ton and headed for the Knife Lake country toward the northeast. Many of those first portages and camps are all but lost
now in thousands of wilderness memories, but there were certain experiences that still stand out, such as the night we came
to Knife. There I was filled with such wonder and delight as
I had never known.

It was sunset when we crossed the last portage around the
rapids of the Knife River and stood at last on the shores of the
lake itself. A golden glow lay over the water and over our
minds as well, and as I looked down that dusky waterway for
the first time, saw its rocky islands floating in the distance
against the haze of high terrain to the east, I was aware of a
fusion with the country, an overwhelming sense of completion in which all my hopes and experiences seemed crystallized
into one shining vision.

The loons were calling, I can hear them yet, echoes rolling
back from the shores and from unknown lakes across the
ridges until the dusk seemed alive with their music. This untamed sound, the distances, the feeling of mystery and adventure filled me with joy and elation. Here to my young mind
was the threshold of the wild, and what Kipling meant in

Something lost beyond the ranges.

I know now why children are sometimes seized with the
necessity of expressing their joy in violent physical activity,
why they dance and run and climb and tumble until utter

weariness makes them pause. And so it was with me that night on Knife. I felt I must run and shout, somehow embrace those far horizons and all the new sounds and smells and sensations that were mine. But because I was more than a child, a young man who could carry a pack and a canoe, I stood still and hid my emotions like the rest. It was then, however, that I entered into a life filled with the desire to explore the hinterlands of the north.

We threw the packs into the canoes, pushed down the lake, got out the trolling line with its big Skinner spoon and trailed it behind us. We had gone perhaps a mile when I felt a tremendous tug. We stopped paddling and with excitement I pulled in the fish I had hooked. It was big and heavy and fought me all the way. After a time there was a flash of silver below the canoe as a huge trout came out of the blue-green depths. It was shining and powerful and swam in wide circles beneath me. When it was tired, I brought it close to the canoe, reached down and slipped my hand into its gill. With a heave, I lifted it out and then it lay before me huge and glistening, cold and hard, its red gills opening and closing slowly. We stared at it in amazement, stroked its sides. None of us had ever seen a fish like this. Here was a fish of the north, different from the little brook trout in the creeks back home, and from the sunfish in the pond. This to us was food for explorers and men of the wilds.

It was almost dark now and the shores loomed vaguely before us. We glided by an island, nosed into the bank and found we could land without difficulty. Because the shore was steep and covered with ledges and boulders, we carried the packs up to the top of the island to where it was level and smooth beneath a pine. Swiftly we kindled a fire between the rocks, pitched the tent and laid out our gear. The trout was broiled over the coals and with strong tea and bread we ate it ravenously. Around us was the firelight, above, the protecting branches of the pines. We lay there and watched the golden tracery of boughs and were content.

In the morning we discovered we had pitched our tent on a flat ledge of rock commanding a splendid view down the lake. Above the water some fifteen feet, it was like sitting on the prow of a ship. The water was clear, the rocks and trees freshly scrubbed and immaculate. The land seemed clean, new, unused.

Across from our camp to the north, and on the Canadian side of the border, was a stand of pine; beyond that, as far as we knew, were thousands of miles of wild country to roam and explore, an unbroken expanse clear to the arctic. To the south of us, on the American side, much of it had been logged for almost a hundred miles to the shores of Lake Superior; but to us, on this voyage of discovery, it still seemed unravished and unspoiled. As I sat there I felt the country's bigness, its space and unexplored distances.

The days that followed were full of wonderment. The spell that was upon us continued, and all we saw was colored by its mood. Once we came to a little bay between Knife and Ottertrack where the pines and spruces were mirrored so perfectly we lost the shores in their reflections. Paradise Harbor we named it, for so it seemed to us.

A few miles down the lake and across from the cliffs, we found a waterfall tumbling down a smooth shelf covered with shimmering moss. We sat beside it in a clump of old cedars and marveled at the lacework of white and translucent green against the rocks. Never for a moment was the color the same, never for an instant unchanging. One of us called it Bridal Veil Falls. Behind us were cliffs with stiff, marching stands of spruce, bare faces of ledge painted in orange and black, and down the lake were the canyonlike narrows all remember, who have ever paddled Ottertrack.

Then we came to Saganaga, saw it first through a channel like an open gate, glimpsed its immensities of blue toward the east. This we called the Gateway to Saganaga, and to us it was a pathway to the unknown. Before us was the miracle of open and distant horizons. We passed through the channel, entered the great body of water with awe, coasted between rounded islands that looked as though they had been trimmed with gigantic shears, moved at last into Cache Bay and heard before us the thunder of a great falls.

We saw the mist and felt the power of the undertow and cautiously crept along the shore until we found the portage. The air was alive with the thunder. Halfway over we dropped our canoes and packs and stopped to gaze into a plunging fury of white and gold. On the return trip, we crawled out to a pinnacle of rock at the very brink of the falls, lay there look-ing down into the maelstrom below. Silver Falls, this was the entrance to Saganagons, a waterway we would follow to still newer adventures in the north.

Traversing the lake, we rounded a long slender peninsula almost cutting it in two, found its outlet and knew again the exaltation of spouting rocks and rapids with a roaring canyon down below. We portaged along a knife edge of rock with white water on either side, and pitched our tent on a ledge above the tumult.

Down the gloomy Kawnippi, on a day full of clouds and storm, we found another river with many rapids and were spewed at last into Sturgeon Lake with its white glaciated shores. Then down the storied Maligne with its crumbling dams of the Dawson Expedition and, finally, among the is-lands of Lac la Croix, we found the Indian paintings on a stark cliff above the water's edge and sat there in wonder-ment trying to understand. We passed the Indian village, went down the Snake and up into the country of the Beaverhouse and Quetico lakes with their great stands of timber.

Until then all had been magic and mystery. When it stormed we gloried in thunder and lightning. When the waves rolled, we were one with the whitecaps and the wind. When the skies were alive with northern lights and the stars close enough to touch, we quoted "Spell of the Yukon" and were sourdoughs of '98.

Not another soul did we see during all this time, for the

country, then, had not been discovered by fishermen or canoeists. We came to believe we were the only ones in the entire Quetico-Superior and became so imbued with the feeling that this wilderness belonged to us alone, it was a distinct shock one day to see a tent pitched on a beach across the lake. As we neared we saw it was no ordinary *voyageur's* camp, for the tent was large and a big bateau with a motor was drawn up on the shore. Oil drums were scattered about and big trees had been felled. Instead of a small rock fireplace near the water, a stove had been set up. Smoke was coming out of its chimney and beside it stood a man with a white apron tied around his waist.

Two other men came out of the timber behind the beach and all three came down to meet us. Much older than we were, they wore heavy beards, were dressed in stag pants and lumberjack boots. We looked at them with something akin to apprehension, for to us they seemed foreign and out of place. Intruders in our world of dreams, they did not belong to the land we had found.

"Come on in, boys," said the man with the white apron, "how about some coffee?"

We could not resist, so paddled ashore, pulled our canoes up beside the bateau and sat down on a log near the stove. The cook gave each of us a mug of steaming coffee and some fresh doughnuts, but we said little—for how could they know about the glory of the new country we had come through? How could they understand about Paradise Harbor, Silver

Falls—or how we felt that first night at Knife? Much better if we could act like lumberjacks or timber cruisers doing men's work. So, with bravado and somewhat cheered by the coffee, we talked of timber stands we had seen, of rocks and prospecting, though we knew nothing of such things, trying to appear as hardbitten and nonchalant as they.

But they knew better and to them we were just a party of boys out for a holiday, striplings who knew nothing about the country or what it was really for. These practical men told us they were cruising timber and that all the magnificent pine around the lakes was destined for the mills.

We had seen the pines the evening before, when the level rays of the sun had streaked them with gold, and that morning had watched as the white mist all but hid them from view. Somehow I felt I should tell them what we had seen and how we felt, but the words stuck in my throat. To them the trees were already cut and in the rafts, the rapids sluiced and the lakes dammed for the spring drives to Fort Francis and the mills. They were so matter-of-fact about what they were doing, there seemed no question but that the logging was right.

We listened with horror, could see as they talked the beautiful sandy beach strewn with debris, the tall pines down, the rapids choked with logs. The very thought of it seemed unreal. Suddenly we were confused and "something lost beyond the ranges" sounded childish in the face of what these men could do.

We thanked them, went back to the canoes and pushed off. "Have a good time," called the cook, "and don't get lost."

I laughed as gaily as I could, but from that moment we looked at the shores, the portage trails, the rapids and the rocks, and saw them all with sadness as though we were saying goodbye. But after a time and many miles away we began to forget; and once more the joy that had been ours when we first came into the country returned.

Having no particular route or schedule to keep, we were free as the wind and chose lakes and rivers that ran in the general direction we wanted to go. Everywhere there was challenge and poetry, everywhere the kind of country we had left behind. Moose were plentiful then and we saw them often in the beaver flowages and in the swampy bays of lakes. Once when paddling down a shore we saw a cow and a calf in the water feeding on lily pads; and, while we watched, a great bull charged down the hillside behind us and struck the shallows nearby with an enormous splash that rocked the canoes. We pushed away swiftly and for a time we thought the bull was pursuing us, but when he reached deep water he turned and went back to the shore free of the flies which no doubt had been tormenting him.

Another time we paddled up to a bull which was facing the bank. It was dusk and by moving only when the animal's head was submerged we were able to get close enough to hit its rump a resounding smack with the paddle. So violent was the reaction of the startled animal that we almost upset as it reared and plunged desperately to get out of the muck and onto the shore.

Once paddling down a narrow winding creek, we rounded a bend and directly before us saw a mother bear and two cubs. The mother lay astride a log over the water, the cubs in the shallows beneath her. For a moment we watched as she played a game of catch-my-paw-if-you-can. Then she discovered us and the water flew as the three of them left the creek and charged over the bank.

Countless times we watched beaver around their houses and were delighted when they slapped their tails in warning. One morning an otter family dove and bobbed around our canoes, hissed and coughed and cavorted without fear. Ducks skittered constantly before us and once, going through a rice bed, a flock of mallards took to the air and we heard the whisper of their wings as they left for other feeding grounds.

We made new camps almost every night, came to know strange chains of lakes and their connecting rivers, shores with uncruised stands of pine, valleys of aspen and birch, flowages, and meandering creeks with beaver dams across them. Sometimes we left the waterways and struck off across country, over rocky ridges and enormous muskegs, to find new lakes that were not shown on the maps.

When at last the trip was over, we landed at the little dock at Winton where we had begun our cruise long before. Our packs were worn, the canoes no longer new, and our clothes patched and in tatters. We stood at the water's edge, looked down the lake and thought of the many miles we had paddled and of all we had seen. It was not goodbye for us, but the beginning of many expeditions in the future—for we had glimpsed a freedom that must be tasted time and again.

CHAPTER 3

THE WELL

WHY DIG for water when the lake was crystal clear and uncontaminated, billions of gallons of it at my very door? Why go to all that work when there was no need? Furthermore, digging would make an ugly scar, inevitably change the immediate area, disturb flowers and mosses. I put off the project time and again, but always in the back of my mind was the thought that some day, in spite of all the arguments against it, I should dig a little well, not an elaborate affair by grace of blasting, drilling, and concrete, but a primitive one, merely a little hand-dug hole in the ground with its source seepage from the lake, and beside it a cup at the end of a stick for scooping up a drink.

I felt I wanted to go through the motions of getting water as settlers had done. It would feel good to go back to the days, not only of my own boyhood, but to the youth of the race, back even to the days of pre-history when man first abandoned his nomadic wanderings and settled down on a plot of ground near some water supply he had chosen for his own.

Around the walls of such a well, I argued, would grow lichens, liverworts, mosses, and flowers in far greater profusion than anywhere else, for in its very breathing would be life. In a sense it would be a shrine, a place of contemplation and revery, a refuge where I could watch and listen, dedicated to the entire concept of simplicity.

There would be practical advantages too, for no matter how warm the days of midsummer, down close to the water table it would be cold as ice. There I could store perishables and keep them fresh. True, the lake was cold, but not quite cold enough to keep such luxuries from spoiling during July and August.

The pool in the bottom of the well would mirror my face as I leaned over it, would reflect not only me but my thoughts as well, a polished jewel deep down in the rocks, to make me glad.

And so the die was cast and I began to look around for a proper place to dig. A low spot at the very base of the point, a little hollow surrounded by big pines with a deeper depression in between them seemed a possible site. Not thirty feet from the water's edge were three trees growing in a gravel bank between two ledges of sloping greenstone. If I could get down below the level of the lake, water would surely seep through the sand and gravel. While it would not be a spring in the true sense of the word, nevertheless it would flow and be cooled beneath the roots of the pines. There would always be shade and I pictured it with the scars of digging healed—a tiny, protected pool sheltered by great buttressing roots and held in their embrace. I walked around the spot many times, examined it from every angle, for there must be no mistake. Only fifty feet from the cabin, and beside the trail running to the end of the point, this surely was the place.

One morning I took a spade, an iron bar, and an axe, stepped down into the hollow between the pines and carefully sliced through the duff where I was to dig, lifted off a six-inch cover of pine needles, bits of half-decayed bark, little branches and caribou moss—the gathering of a century or more, laid the mat to one side. Below the duff was a foot of humus interlaced with roots and fibers, all that had accumulated since the retreat of the glacial ice some ten thousand years ago. This, too, I removed and laid to one side. Below all of this were boulders, most of them small, lying loosely one on top of the other. I lifted each one out and placed it beside the pile of humus. Those at the very top I kept separate, for some had mosses and lichens attached to their surfaces. Those further down were black with the seepage from the humus above.

By the time I had worked my way down several feet, I ran into ledge—solid greenstone sloping to a V in the exact center of the hole, no gravel, no sand, only solid rock, and dry as dust with not a sign of seepage or damp. I would have to go down at least two more feet to reach the level of the lake but that was now impossible. For a time I stared at the rock, brushed away the dry earth to be sure, felt of the ledge with my hands. It was cold, but there was no sign of water and with this formation there never would be.

I replaced the stones exactly as I had found them and placed the humus over the top of the hole, then smoothed and patted the round cap of duff into place. No one would know what I had done or how the greenstone looked underneath. No one had seen it but me.

My disappointment was keen, however, for this had seemed the ideal place, and long before the day I began to work, I had pictured the well there. Those three great pines almost meeting overhead seemed the perfect setting, as though grown for the express purpose of sheltering a water hole.

I picked up my tools and walked down the shore toward the beach at the end of the bay. On the way I examined several other sites where the water might have a chance of seeping in from the lake, for long ago I had decided I did not want a deep well. Each was the same, however, a solid ledge of greenstone underneath, not a one with a direct connection of sand and gravel with the floor of the lake itself.

At last I found myself down at the beach and in the clump of cedars behind it. Among them lay a confusion of moss-covered boulders which could mean only one thing, that long ago, perhaps several hundred years, the little bay had been the outlet of a clear stream bringing down water from the hills to the lake. I could see it now, swirling over its boulder-strewn mouth, rolling the gravel over and over and carrying the sand out into the bay where in time it washed back to make the beach. Today there is no evidence of the river, not even a tiny rivulet, nor could I hear the sound of running water, but as I studied the terrain, it seemed as though there must be something underneath, some flow following the ancient drainage pattern toward the lake. There was no evidence of ledge. The old outlet must be deep in sand and gravel below the moss-covered boulders that lay everywhere.

I chose a place that was lower than the rest. Leaning near was an old aspen two feet through at the butt, and tilted by the wind, but still growing. There were young cedars around it and a big spruce to one side. Again I removed the boulders of the surface, careful not to disturb the mosses and lichen that covered them. Just below the surface were other rocks black with muck from the seepage. I took them up one by one and soon had a big pile of greenstone, hematite, granite, and schist. None were large, and all lay loosely one upon the other. There they had been since the days of the ice age and as I had seen them at the forefront of glaciers in Alaska and the West. They had not changed their positions very much, had lain in the stream bed while migrating tribes crossed the ice of Bering Strait to work their long way into the interior of the North American continent. They were there when the pyramids were built long before the birth of Christ, and when the *voyageurs* came through on fur trading and exploring expeditions in the Northwest, and when this country of the Quetico-Superior was first settled.

Down I went, foot by foot, until it became increasingly difficult to lift each boulder to the top. At four feet, I began to see the end of my work, still no sand or gravel, but again a slanting piece of ledge, the old greenstone that had stopped me before. If it extended across the hole, it would be the end of any hope of a well. I lay there looking into the darkness of the hole I had made and, as my eyes became accustomed to the murk, I saw the ledge clearly. It was green in color, and hard and wet. At least it was wet, but again there was no flow, no seepage.

Then a movement caught my eye, a tiny spurting of water coming out of what looked like a small crevice, not more than a quarter of an inch in width. Like a severed artery it spurted, ebbed, and flowed and even as I watched with amazement and delight the hole I had made began to fill with water. A spring coming through the native rock; what more could I wish for?

For a long time I watched as the water grew deeper and deeper. It was muddy now for the stones had been covered with muck. I reached down as far as I could with my hands and the water was cold as ice. I loosened a few more rocks beside the crevice and when I could find no more, drew myself out of the hole and sat there gloating in the sunshine. No more than four feet down, it was deep enough for my purpose. The hole itself was about eighteen inches across and thanks to the positions of the boulders, it was faced with them as though I had built a wall around it. A tiny pool it would be, just a symbol of a well, but in time the water would clear and all the things I had thought about would come to pass.

Around the top of the hole were several large, jagged rocks. I filled in the places between them with the stones I had moved and placed those covered with moss on top. When I had finished, I gathered pine needles and scraps of cedar twigs and sprinkled them around to complete the illusion. No one would know what I had done. I then went back to the cabin to fashion a scoop. A four-foot stick of hazel with a tin cup fastened securely to one end, and a hook for hanging it on a branch, was all I needed in the way of equipment. Then searching the shoreline for a flat stone to cover the opening, I returned to the well. There was now a foot of water in the hole and I scooped it up and sprinkled the stones all around. In time, and with constant wettings, many things would grow and thrive there that until now had little chance of survival. After several complete emptyings of the well, the water began to clear, but I knew it would take a day or more before it was entirely settled. I took the flat rock and fitted it over the opening as best I could. It was snug except for one little spot. I realized I must fix that or a mouse or a frog might get through, fall into the well and if I happened to be gone, the water would go bad.

It was late when I finished and the hermit thrushes were

calling. I sat there and listened, and it seemed to me their music was even lovelier than before. Somehow their limpid, bubbling notes seemed part of the tiny trickle spurting out of the ledge below. When it was too dark to see any more, I picked up the iron bar, the shovel, and the axe and returned to the cabin. Mine was the good feeling of all men who had found water of their own.

One morning I lifted off the cover and stared down into the well. The water was dark and shining and after a time I could faintly see my own visage, but then the water moved and no sooner did I discern my reflection than it disappeared. Something was down there moving slowly across the pool. Then I saw what it was, a frog floating on the surface. It lay there quietly, its golden eyes upon me.

"Hello, Rana," I said, "and how does it feel to go swimming in my well?"

The little creature blinked its eyes and one hind foot moved gently, setting up ripples which lost themselves against the walls.

Rana was of an ancient race, one of the amphibia, predating man by untold millions of years. His forebears had left the slime of some primordial sea for the land and had developed lungs instead of gills to use the oxygen of the air.

We studied each other and I wondered what primal reactions were running through its amphibious nerve centers as it lay there watching. The same life flowed in Rana as in me. We were brothers under the skin. It knew nothing whatever of

37

such things as the atomic arms race, or missiles, nationalism, or self-determination, but it did know something about the feel of water and mist and the sound of waves and of rain, something about shadows and the threat of a long sharp bill of some heron wading the shallows, or the swift flash of a pike from the deeps.

Loren Eiseley once spoke of his meeting with a frog.

"Yet whenever I see a frog's eye low in the water warily ogling the shoreward landscape, I always think inconsequentially of those twiddling mechanical eyes that mankind manipulates nightly from a thousand observatories. Someday, with a telescopic lens an acre in extent, we are going to see something not to our liking, some looming shape outside there across the great pond of space.

"Whenever I catch a frog's eyes I am aware of this, but I do not find it depressing. I stand quite still and try hard not to move or lift a hand since it would only frighten him. And standing thus, it finally comes to me that this is the most enormous extension of vision of which life is capable; the projection of itself into other lives. This is the lonely, magnificent power of humanity. It is far more than any spatial adventure, the supreme epitome of the reaching out."

I thought of his words as I looked down at Rana. There it was just as before. I stared into its eyes and it into mine. I could project myself but Rana could not.

I reached down into the well, picked up the frog and gently set it down on a small moss-covered boulder nearby. For a moment it sat there, then unerringly headed for the lakeshore. A final jump and it was out of sight. The marsh grass moved several times and then it was still. Rana was back home, safe in some crevice between the rocks. Already its adventure was forgotten. All that mattered now was the wash of the waves, the swaying of the cattails above it. I went back to the well, plugged the little opening where the frog had come through, and placed the flat rock carefully on top.

All during the spring and summer, the water level stayed high, but toward fall it dropped until there was no spurting out of the crevice. To me, watching every day, that crevice became an indicator of the condition of the land, for here was a tiny artery, part of the vast circulatory system of the entire area. If the surge of water was pulsating and strong, the water table was high and all life benefited. If it slowed to a barely perceptible seepage, the woods were thirsty.

My well was a symbol of all that wells had meant to man, their fullness often a matter of life or death to those who depended upon them. In the southwest it was they who made the cliff dwellers leave their pueblos. In the Near East, they determined the fate of ancient civilizations. Drouth and thirst were more feared than disease or war.

The following spring, the water was almost two feet in depth for there had been plenty of snow. It was just a year since I found the well and in that time it had lost its newness. Mosses and lichens had grown around it and wild flowers had come in: gold thread, Linnaea, blue violets, and tiny white ones. The mosses were luxuriant and lush on the nearby rocks, and star-shaped heads reached toward the light. In between the rocks sphagnum grew, pink and light green, thriving in the standing water there. Dwarf dogwood had sprung up, the four-clustered leaves sending pale green petals between them.

I knelt and scooped up a dipperful and drank deeply. It was clear and cold, tasted faintly of sphagnum and the rocks that hemmed it in, for it was of the earth and open woods and springs that had never known imprisonment or care. This was water of the wilderness.

The little trail leading back from the beach was already well worn, so swiftly do one's footsteps compact moss and soil. The path ends at the big spruce where the cup hangs. Only a foot wide, should I never return, this trail would nevertheless be visible for a long time, so fragile is the earth.

CHAPTER 4

HUNTING MOON

When the hunting moon of October first appears, it is big and orange and full of strange excitement. Then it is at its best; later it pales, but those first few moments are moments of glory.

On one such night we decided to climb the high hill north of the town of Ely and there, with miles of wilderness extending toward the east, watch from the first brightening of the sky until the moon was high and full. It was a spur-of-the-moment decision, something unplanned, and the time actually stolen, for there were many other things to do which seemed more vital. Hastily, and almost with a sense of guilt, we donned boots and jackets and drove around the head of the lake to the base of a long ridge beside the Echo Trail, arriving a little breathlessly just before dusk.

The leaves were still in gorgeous color, sheltered maples still flaming, the ground cover a carpet of reds, browns, and yellows, but that evening it was the aspen that were most beautiful of all. As we climbed the slope and threaded our way through the jackpine, we had no hint of what was to come; but, as we emerged on an open shelf two thirds of the way to the summit, we looked down on a tall stand of aspen in a valley below and in the approaching dusk their color was old gold and peach, a soft diffusion of warmth we had never seen before. So lovely was the sight, we almost forgot the real purpose of our climb and that the steepest part was still to be scaled if we were to see the moon come up. As we climbed, we turned time and again to look below, to bathe our senses in a glow that was already melting into the dark.

We reached the lookout point at last, a bare glaciated knob at the highest and most exposed pinnacle of the ridge. Some hardy maples still held a few brilliant leaves, but a scrub oak in a protected crevice flaunted its mahogany in triumph over the gales. To the south the lake was tinted with the sunset, and beyond were the twinkling lights of town. As dusk descended, the water turned to wine, then to black, and the molten gold below faded into the darkness of the valley. The stage was set and we watched the ridge to the east.

It was then we became conscious of light to the north and

within minutes the aurora began to play, first a vague shimmering curtain, faintly tinged with rose and yellow, wavering across the sky. This was something we had not expected, but there it was, an almost hesitant display to be sure, but northern lights just the same. It disappeared as swiftly as it had come and again we watched the horizon to the east for the first telltale brightening. Then in a sudden explosion of color the aurora returned and now there were several drifting curtains, blending and shaking and crossing one another until the entire sky was a confusion of diaphanous veils finally converging until they met in a swirling mass directly overhead. A fitting prelude to the rise of the hunting moon.

Again it was dark, far darker than before. So absorbed had we been in the northern lights, we almost missed the first hint of the moon in the east. Now in a dark notch of the hills had come a change, a barely perceptible one, but as we watched the brightness increased and the notch became plainly outlined. There seemed to be a boiling and stirring of vapors such as one sees at dawn below a falls or rapids.

A slender scimitar of orange sliced through the mist, first only its thin upper edge, then the whole of its rounded rim. The full moon was trembling and pulsating as it pushed and struggled upward and away from the haze which enveloped it. Now it was half, then three quarters. The mists were subsiding, slipping away from their tenuous hold on the lower rim. At last the moon was free, an oval, glowing ball of orange; the hunting moon of October.

A great horned owl hooted down in the valley, hoo-hoo-oooooo-hoo-hooooooooo. It would wait until the hollows were silvered with light, then glide through the trees on cushioned wings. Birds would stop their cheeping, rabbits and mice freeze in their tracks. All forms of life would wait until the danger was gone. This was a night of hunting not only for the owl, but for all predators in the north—including man the fiercest of them all.

The moon was losing color swiftly and climbing high. Paling into yellow now, it would soon be silvery white. The tops of the aspen far below were washed with gold and silver. By midnight the entire valley would be almost as light as day.

I studied the moon through my field glasses, its vague continental masses, its mountain ranges, charted, named, and well known. Somewhere on its surface was a man-made thing. For the first time in history, it had been touched by a machine. Echoes and messages were bounced off its surface as boys might carom a ball in play, and now we talked of sending men there and I had no doubt but with our ingenuity, it would be possible in the not-too-distant future.

Reach the hunting moon? The very idea was preposterous. Surely, I thought, this cannot happen but I knew that sooner or later we would accomplish the impossible. Crossing a quarter of a million miles of space meant little to rockets traveling at supersonic speeds. But somehow, on this night, all of this seemed wrong and out of place, like trying to evaluate a painting by analyzing its pigments, or a symphony by calculating wave lengths of sound. For me the moon's true meaning would be what I had felt and seen as it rose above the hills.

The moon was almost white now and all around us colored leaves and surfaces were beginning to shine and glisten. Moonlight on a frosted leaf belonged to the world of the intangibles. And with that I was content, for though man might soon survey the shining satellite, he could never probe its spiritual impact. Hunting moons would come and go and men watching would always be moved by their beauty and mystery to ponder deeper meanings. New knowledge could, however, lead to a greater perspective based on truth and understanding and an eventual flowering of mind and spirit in relationship to the universe as a whole.

We built our fire, a little one of small sticks and bits of bark, put on the coffee pot. The tiny blaze illumined the grey caribou moss on the rocks, picked out a patch of scarlet sumac we had not seen before and some bearberry running like a red scar along a crevice in the ledge.

I remembered the time of another hunting moon far to the north, so far that it came a month earlier. We were camped on a rocky promontory on Black Lake between Wollaston and Lake Athabasca in the far reaches of Canada's Northwest. It had been a day of long portages, muskeg, and fighting the wind, and we were weary as only men can be after traveling from dawn to dusk. There had been no sun all day, only dark and lowering clouds. We pitched our tents on a flat spit of glaciated rock close to the mouth of a river and at the beginning of a long portage around a series of rapids. In the morning we would carry the canoes three miles across a sandy plain grown with jackpine, followed by another portage of over a mile and a half to a boggy lake on the way to Stony Rapids Post of the Hudson's Bay Company at the east end of Lake Athabasca.

I remembered getting the fire under way and the pots on to boil while the others busied themselves making their beds and putting gear and food under cover for a possible blow and rain during the night. Several Indian canoes passed along the far shore. There were five all told, a hunting party going after moose or caribou. The canoes crept along the darkening shore perhaps a mile away and though the Indians could see our fire, they paid not the slightest heed. They, too, were late and heading for some campsite down the lake, doing what men had always done in the north with the coming of the hunting moon.

There, I thought, could be men of the ice age, or men of Europe, or Siberia, thousands of years ago. They were the men who stayed along the edge of the ice, followed it first south, then north with its retreat. Ten thousand years is short in the history of a race. Here in the far north, with the hunting moon, life went on as of old.

The canoes disappeared behind an island, and the far shore blazed with sudden light as the setting sun found a rift in the clouds. Beyond the island, the canoes reappeared and were black against the glow, the figures of the paddlers plain.

Though there was still much to do, everyone left his work to join me. We were oblivious of time, watching a tableau of the past. The shore became a streak of livid gold against the black of the horizon and before it crept the line of canoes heading for their rendezvous.

A pair of loons flew overhead, their calls dying in the distance. They, too, saw the line of canoes silhouetted against the golden shore, but only we could wonder at its haunting beauty. The Indians paddled on in the last wash of light and warmth, threaded their way along a fringe of burning grasses, moving without effort. Theirs, too, was the ancient response to a brief moment of light and glory.

The sun sank below the break in the clouds, and the bar of orange light was slowly brushed with black. One by one the canoes slipped into the dusk and were gone. For a time we stood there held by the spell, for we too had slipped into the dusk with the Stone Age hunters of the north.

We ate our supper beside the fire, crept into our bags and went to sleep. Later I awoke and came out of the tent. The east end of the lake was brightening and I watched another hunting moon of orange climb into the sky and flood the water with its brilliance. Here, too, a moonrise had had its prelude, a prelude as startling as the northern lights we had just seen. The moon made its path across the lake and I knew to the west it was shining down the whole length of Athabasca, as it was to the north on Great Slave, and over the barren expanses of Great Bear south of the Arctic Coast.

47

Two years later we were back in the north at the time of another hunter's moon. It had been a period of storm and cold without sunsets, moonrises, or northern lights to cheer our journey. We were above Great Bear in the Dismal Lakes country and I had stolen away from the rest and walked alone on a barren hillside. Before me and all around was the bleak and windswept country of the Arctic slope. To the east a few miles was the partly frozen Coppermine River and Bloody Falls where the Eskimo were surprised by a party of Indians and massacred to the last, the route of Samuel Hearne looking for a gateway to the Arctic Sea. Father Rouvière had named the lake before me, had stood perhaps on this same rise looking at the hills to the north, and at the slender sand spit which almost cut the lake in two. Sir John Franklin had come this way, and Charles Camsell. This was land they had known and explored.

Eskimo country, here roamed the caribou, the musk ox, and the barren-ground grizzly. Soon the tundra would be white with snow, but now it was a mosaic of color with cranberries and bilberries like jewels among the mosses and lichens. The vines had turned to brilliant red, dwarf willow and birch to orange. The flowers were gone but here and there a few held bravely to their faded petals. A tiny willow no more than three inches high still had a withered and wind-beaten tuft of fuzz covering its single catkin. It had flowered late and during the short arctic summer barely had time to bloom before the

48

coming of the cold. There was snow in the air and the wind from the arctic ice was bitter and raw.

A small animal scurried past, a lemming or a ground squirrel. A flock of snow buntings drifted by, made a wide swing, dropped like leaves of brown and white beside me. Soon they would be back home in the Quetico-Superior two thousand miles away and I would watch them skim over the snow, dash into some patch of weeds to feed on the harvest their bodies and wings had shaken from the stalks. I would remember then and think of the barrens far away.

As I looked toward the low range of hills marking the divide between Rouvière and the Dismal Lakes, I thought how well named it was by the explorers working up the shallow rapids from Coppermine to Great Bear, how fiercely desolate it could be until the sun shone or the moon came out. I wanted to see those barren hills shining again in the light, the waters below a path of silver, but this joy was denied me. Knowing the tundra at the coming of the cold, I knew that as far as it extended from Hudson Bay to the Arctic Islands this time was past. When the moon came again it would be a winter moon shining on a land that had changed little since the days of the great ice, a bleakness without trees, destined perhaps never to know more than the tiny plants growing through the half-frozen muck above the permafrost. Except for a few short weeks, it was always cold; and underneath was the ice that determined what might survive. Few would ever see this land

and few would ever come of their own accord to live.

Here, I thought, might be the last stand of man in North America. Should total war come, survivors here, unaware of what had happened down below, would struggle as they had always done, living off the land, building their shelters, and dreaming the long dreams that once again might mean man's rise from the primitive.

A movement beside me and I was back again beside our little fire on the ledge. It was time to go, for in spite of the moonlight, the trail would be rough. We had seen a vale of aspen in the old gold of dusk, a lake turning rose with the sunset, northern lights flaming across the heavens as a prelude to the moonrise itself. In the embers of our tiny flame I had remembered a night in the Athabasca country and on the tundra beyond the Arctic Circle. All this and the calling of a horned owl in the space of a few stolen hours.

CHAPTER 5

CRANBERRY BOG

I PUSHED the canoe into the edge of the bog where a heavy mat of sphagnum and heather hung out over the water, tried the footing cautiously. Still too soft to hold my weight I cruised along the shore until I found a beaver channel, turned into the passageway and went up as far as I could. Freshly gnawed aspen twigs floated in the water and at the end was a well-beaten beaver runway leading toward a patch of trees a hundred yards away. Getting food was a difficult thing, now that the fringe of birch and aspen had been cut all along the shore. The canal would get longer and longer in the attempt to reach trees and finally would come to the end of the bog.

The canoe, supported by heavy muskeg on both sides, was steady now. I tested the mat, stepped out, and though it went down, it was strong enough to support me. Very carefully now, and using my paddle as a crutch, I walked ahead watching the deep black holes between the hummocks. The muskeg lying over the bog was springy and at times seemed as though it must surely give way and let me down into the water and muck underneath. Labrador tea, swamp laurel, Andromeda, sedges, and sphagnum, all woven through with the tiny grass-like stems of cranberry; here was a stable ecological community, more ancient perhaps than the forests surrounding it.

Running across the bog like a network were the trails of moose and deer following, perhaps, those made originally by the caribou of long ago. I followed one, knowing the animals avoided soft places where they might mire, soon found what I was looking for, a patch of bright red berries embedded in the moss. I settled down on a spongy rise and began to pick, and soon my gallon pail was full to the brim.

How beautiful they were, full firm, and ripe. This was truly fruit of the north with a range extending from the northern tier of states as far as the arctic. Other fruits may be as typically American but none has such a continental sweep. The cherries, the plums, and the apples might resemble one another slightly in taste, but not the cranberry. It has a distinctive character of its own and a flavor seemingly compounded of the qualities of its environment. When you eat cranberries you savor the dank pungence of the muskeg itself,

those great mats of heather and moss covering once open glacial ponds and even the bays of larger lakes.

On the tundras west of Hudson Bay are hundreds of thousands of water-filled depressions, looking little different than
they did when the great ice mass retreated several thousand
years ago. From the air there seems to be more water than
land, but a slow change is taking place, the invasion of all
these gathered waters by muskeg. Each pond is rimmed with
green at its edge, with orange and bronze near the shore. The
land is a great mosaic of it, and stippled throughout with blue.
Eventually the muskeg will win up there as it has already
won to the south and the waters of today will only be outlines
of what they once were. If there are trees around them,
seedlings will take root on the bogs, will march out from the
shores and the little lakes will be gone. All the way from New
England to the middle west, and north almost as far as one
can go, this is taking place.

The cranberry marsh I was on was no different than the
rest, for scattered through it were these little trees, some of
them very old because of the cold acidity of the medium in
which they grew. Once I cut such a tree, a two-inch black
spruce, counted the rings and found it was over a hundred
years of age. Along the edge were alder and a stand of red
ozier dogwood whose stems were flaming red. On one hummock higher than the rest, and supported no doubt by a boulder or a deposit of glacial moraine, grew a tiny gnarled birch
trying to hold its own. Farther inland was a growth of dwarf

birch, an impenetrable tangle no more than three or four feet in height, the same dwarf birch that grows only a few inches during its lifetime south of the Arctic Coast. Another place had a small aspen and two tiny spruce, so fragile they looked more like ferns than trees.

As the bog filled with vegetation, more and more invaders would work their way out into it from the surrounding highland forests, their roots weaving themselves into the mat of muskeg, their stems and leaves settling onto the surface, until it was dry enough to support other forms of life. I looked at the forest of the far shore. It had been waiting for thousands of years but there was plenty of time. It would take more thousands to cover the whole bay. The deeper part of the lake might never be conquered, but the shallow parts were doomed.

Flying over this land, one can see these ancient lakes and ponds, the ones that have lost their battle. Though long overgrown, their outlines stand clear, their bays and islands marked by the relentless muskeg. Each year the forest consolidates its victory a little more and in time even this evidence of the old shorelines will disappear as the once water-filled depressions become timbered valleys. Only in the land of the permafrost, where there is little drainage, do shallow waters have any relative permanence, but even there the muskeg moves relentlessly on.

I walked back to the beaver channel and the canoe, emptied

the berries into my pack, rested for a moment and surveyed the bog in its entirety. It was turning to rosy copper now, and around were the waiting ranks of spruce. Once, years ago, I had worked here with a famous paleobotanist. He explained that such a bog is built up over the centuries by the deposition not only of windblown dust and debris, but through the accumulation year by year of plants that have grown and died there. Each year a new layer is formed and if a bog is twenty thousand years of age, there are as many separate strata, one superimposed upon the other, a record of its entire history. Though such plant and animal matter is largely unidentifiable, the pollen grains which have sifted over the area season by season retain their character and tell the story of the surrounding vegetation. By boring down to the very bottom of a bog where it rests on sand, gravel or rock, and studying the cores of peat brought up, he was able to reconstruct the forest history of the area simply by identifying pollen grains.

"Pollen," he explained to me, "is composed of protein surrounded by a tough, indestructible envelope which because of the low oxygen content of the water does not disintegrate. Each pollen grain has a character of its own and can be identified with ease not only in peat which may be ten or twenty thousand years of age, but in beds of coal which may be millions. Every year in the spring when plants flower, there is a veritable rain of golden pollen over the land. Those grains that fall into a marsh settle into the water, sink down into the cold acid muck which forms the peat and, in so doing, put the stamp of their species on each deposit."

To the paleobotanist the tale the pollen told was a dramatic one, of glacial potholes gouged out of solid rock by the ice, or formed by depressions in sand and gravel moraines. First they filled with glacial melt, then came wind-blown debris to settle on the bottom forming soil for water plants, finally the sphagnum and heather working out from the shores until there was only a round spot of blue in the center, a spot that grew smaller and smaller until at last it was closed and the water sealed. The tale those pollen grains told was of phantom forests succeeding one another over the centuries, each forest type indicating changes in climate and cataclysms, long before the advent of civilization.

A layer of predominantly spruce pollen at the very bottom, some twenty feet down, indicated a period of wet and cold following the retreat of the ice; jackpine with little spruce and fir, cold and drouth; white and red pine which was higher than the rest, a time of relative warmth and abundant moisture. By using the radioactivity of carbon as a time scale, Dr. J. E. Potzger found that it took at least 500 years to form a foot of peat and that the bogs of the Quetico-Superior area were often twenty-five thousand years of age.

It was intriguing to sit there in the bog picking cranberries and to know that beneath me, sealed in the black peat, was an indelible record of forest growth, that those forests of the past which had built up the bog to the point where it was to-day, were actually responsible for the fruit I was gathering.

Such an unusual environment could not help but have char-acter, for it was part of all that had gone before. Here was isolation and inaccessibility, a quality which would guarantee the continuance of the bog much longer than the forests around it. This is partly the reason, I have always felt, for the untamed flavor of cranberries and for the fact that even though cultivated widely today under controlled conditions of drainage, they still maintain a certain wildness derived from the peaty depth upon which muskeg thrives.

I like the cranberry best as I saw it before me just after the first frosts, when, through the alchemy of freezing, its sugars are released and the berries seem to be polished and height-ened in color. Then, on their beds of pale-green sphagnum, they glow like rubies with hidden fire. On a day such as this their fragrance is enhanced by the odors of fall until it seems to be a distillation of all that is around them.

My memories of finding cranberries are many and all of them delightful. Once on Crooked Lake I found where they were growing out from a rocky shore and spreading over the water, a floating mat of red and green. All I had to do was paddle close and scoop them into the canoe. Otherwise iden-tical to the berries before me, those on Crooked Lake had adapted themselves to a slightly different physical environ-ment. The roots were laced through sphagnum and heather as always. The last time I was there, the lake was far below where roots could reach the water. I found only a few berries but they were withered and dry. Only in years of high water would they float again.

The Indians and early colonists discovered long ago nothing was so good to eat with meat as the cranberry mixed with maple sugar. When faced with the need of a gift for the king, The Pilgrim Fathers, according to an old story, first talked of sending a shipload of pine timbers, then they thought of choice furs; but these they felt were common gifts without imagination or uniqueness. Whatever was sent must be different, something so typical of the new Massachusetts Bay Colony it could not be duplicated elsewhere.

They remembered then what the Indians had given them that first desperate winter, the red berries of excessive tartness that grew in the bogs around Cape Cod, the berry they called the Crane Berry because of its resemblance, in the stem, to the neck of a crane. Finally they decided to send this unusual fruit, something the king might enjoy as a sauce with the game from his estates. So they gathered basketfuls from the bogs, packed the berries carefully, and shipped them on a swift packet to England. I have wondered at times, if this old story was true, what the berries were like when they reached the king.

I moved farther into the bog. Cranberries were all around me now and I picked only the largest and best, some already dark after the frost, but most firm and red. Not long and my pack basket was almost full. How different, I thought, to be in a bog actually picking them instead of buying them over a counter in a cellophane bag. No one could fully understand until he became part of the environment that produced them, had experienced the adventure of traversing a treacherous stretch of bog with its hidden holes, and known the joy of sitting safely on some dry, firm hummock with the berries in reach.

This was like cutting one's own wood and warming oneself twice in the process, like packing a load across a portage, or doing anything in the out-of-doors yourself. Sprayed, graded berries, grown under ideal conditions, are wonderful—and for those removed from the privilege of seeing them growing in a marsh, they are indeed a gift for a king—but for me there can never be any substitute.

A whiskey jack followed me wherever I went, sure that sooner or later I would leave something behind. Its soft murmurings were fitting music to the work in which I was engaged. It sat on a dead spruce, as silvery-grey as its weathered perch, sat and pondered me quietly. A raven flew overhead in broad, soaring circles watching the tableau below and hoping I would get mired in some bottomless pit. A marsh wren sang gaily from a clump of dwarf birch, cinnamon brown, its tail tilted saucily as it dodged in and out of cover.

Two busy centuries had elapsed since the Pilgrim Fathers made their first important harvest from the native bogs of New England. In all this time the peculiar supremacy of the cranberry had never been questioned and, as holidays have come and gone, it has become more and more firmly entrenched in the affections of the American people. Turkey and cranberry sauce are now synonymous with autumn and color. It has become a tradition, as indigenous as a split hickory fence, Yankee Doodle, or the Suwannee River.

My last pail was full; the whiskey jack and the raven had abandoned their vigils long before. I headed back to the canoe, then paddled to my tent where in a clean, open place under a pine, I dumped the berries onto a blanket and picked out the stems, leaves of heather, shreds of sphagnum. The wind was blowing and I winnowed them until they were clean of chaff and debris.

I decided then to cook some for supper, to taste them while still fresh from the bog, for these, like all others, are at their best when eaten soon after picking. I would fix no more than enough for my evening meal and breakfast as there was no way of carrying the sauce once I began to travel and portage. I chose only the biggest and ripest berries, and, with a little sugar to cut the tartness and enough water to barely cover them, placed the pot over the fire and brought it to a slow, rolling boil.

The berries turned and juices escaped as the largest swelled and burst. The water was red now and I tasted carefully until the flavor was right. The skins were important and to strain them off would be to lose a certain delicacy in taste which I believe is held there, something which seems to me to be the key to the strange essence they possess.

When the sauce was done I dipped a spoon into it, held it to the light to admire its color, for cranberry sauce has a hue all its own, not reddish-orange, purple, or even Chinese red, but a combination perhaps of all of them that color experts, for lack of a better descriptive term, simply call cranberry and let it go at that. Long ago, artists and craftsmen marveled at the shade and used it in the tinting of beautiful glassware. I brought the pail to the water's edge and set it on a rock to cool.

That evening as I ate my meal and relished my treat I could see the bog across the bay. It was misty now and a flock of mallards wheeled low across it on their way to some rice fields nearby. With each spoonful I could smell that bog, feel its resilience, and see the berries there. All this was in my pack basket, and during the winter ahead I would see the bog again and again as it was in the rosy, copper hues of fall, and remember all that had happened there.

CHAPTER 6

WOOD CHANCE

THERE IS nothing that gives a *voyageur* such a sense of security and well-being as having a plentiful supply of good wood near at hand. Protection from wind, a good landing, and a level spot for his tent are important too, but in a country that is often stormy and wet, "the wood chance" as it is called by old-timers all over the bush, is a prime consideration.

My cabin on Listening Point has a good wood chance, plenty of dead aspen and birch, a scattering of pine, and even down cedars along the shore, a limitless supply for years to come. For a time I contented myself with picking up squaw wood as I had always done on the trail, odds and ends of sticks that had dropped from the trees, or windfalls that lay scattered everywhere. Gradually, however, I was forced to travel farther and farther from the cabin to find what I needed. Unlike at temporary camps where there was always enough wood for a night or two, I soon exhausted the immediate supply. One rainy morning I found myself several hundred yards away, completely drenched, before I had picked up enough for my fire.

That experience convinced me that the time had come to lay in a real supply, under the cover of a shelter where it would be safe from rain and snow. There I could forage around among dry chips, shavings, pine knots and debris, and even in the dark find stuff that would burst instantly into flame. The longer I thought about it the sounder the idea seemed to me. For the first time in my life, I would make my wood chance a permanent one.

What was actually in the back of my mind, I believe, was perhaps a certain nostalgia for the woodshed of my boyhood days, a primitive affair full of many kinds of wood, with axes, saws, and canthooks for handling logs, and within it the pungence of split pine, aspen, birch, and cedar. The chickadees were around that woodshed for there were always grubs, insects, and seeds to be found there. Squirrels liked it too, as did chipmunks and mice. It was a gathering and visiting place for all creatures who lived in the surrounding woods and fields.

My woodshed must look as though it had been there for a

long time, which meant I must build it of old logs and boards. I went over the pile of discarded materials left after the completion of the cabin, found some old solid timbers, peeled rafters that were now a golden brown, some boards of silvery grey. There would be no sides, for the wind must blow through it, and the overhanging roof must be wide enough to keep off snow and rain.

I finally picked a level area on a knoll in back of the cabin where I could work in the sunshine with a view over the bay. The footing was good, with only two small aspen to cut. Around it were clumps of white birch and Indian plum and, at one corner, a ragged red pine with a broken top. That pine had character, had survived many catastrophes, would give dignity and stability to the entire project.

Long ago a porcupine had chewed the terminal buds of the pine and had gnawed the bark of the top branches, not once, but time and time again over the years. One shoot had survived, however, and that one branch had finally grown into the scraggly top that now was reaching for the sky. Since that milestone in its career, the tree had done well, but it was scarred and picturesque and would bear the marks of its difficult youth for a long time to come.

I grubbed out several clusters of hazel brush, moved some boulders out of the way, and there before me I could see the structure I would build. About seven by nine with an overhang of two feet all around would make its roof actually eleven by thirteen, large enough for all my needs, no matter how cold or long the winter.

When I told my old friend Bill Langen about my plan, he offered to help me because the logs were solid and heavy and hard to handle alone. For this I was grateful; he knew about wood, shared my feeling for the old days, and had memories of his own. In his boyhood, he had worked in the woods with his father and had learned the art of good axemanship. When his blade bit deep, it went true and with purpose. He had never forgotten those early days or the skills he had learned, and it had colored his sympathy with certain outmoded ideas and a way of life our modern world has all but outgrown. The building of the woodshed to us was the reconstruction of a part of pioneer America and therefore a labor of love.

The foundation logs we chose were as large as we could find and they were supported at the corners by ledge and rocks to keep them off the ground. After we had notched them firmly into place, we set up timbers of the same size on respective corners, squared and steadied them with strips of board, then laid on the four top logs so the slope and over-hang were right. We used rafters of golden balsam every two feet, and covered them with a sheathing of silvery old boards. Only one thing was left to do, finish the roof with something that would shed the rain. Far back in the bush, it would have been broad strips of bark held down with stones or half logs, but here we made a concession to practicality—for back of the cabin we had found part of a roll of dark-green tar paper, just enough to cover it.

For several days we worked with axes, saws, and hammers, days when the leaves, turning gold, were a constant rain of color. This was vital and important work, for out of it would come fires for the future. It would be a storehouse for all the warmth and cheeriness the cabin would know. Here I would work whenever I felt the need, carrying in logs and stumps from the woods, sawing them up, splitting them for future use. On sunny days I could sit on the log pile and look out over the lake, and the birds and squirrels would visit with me. In fact, long before I was through, they discovered what I was up to and seemed as interested and happy with what I was doing as I. Already chips of bark and wood were on the ground with their inevitable harvest of mites and insects that normally would have been hidden to all except the woodpeckers, nuthatches, and chickadees.

I liked the sense of comfortable disorder and growing messiness around me. There is so much of immaculate cleanliness in the homes in which we live, so much of polish, order, and dustlessness, it is good to have a few places where chips and debris lie undisturbed. I looked with satisfaction at the growing collection on the ground around me. It gave me a warm and cozy feeling, and I felt like getting down and burrowing with the squirrels to see what I could find. Underneath and close to the earth itself, the smells would be rich, an antidote to the sterility of modern living.

Woodsheds are almost forgotten now except on some farms and even there they are swiftly being replaced by oil and gas drums. Even in lumber camps, it is no longer profitable to pay a man to cut wood for the stoves. Burning wood instead of fossil fuel is today a luxury no efficiently run outfit can afford. In such operations there is no room for sentiment. But I could afford the joy of burning aspen, birch, and pine for I had nothing to do with cost records, or man-hours of labor. I wanted the work entailed, wanted the feeling that what I was doing was important.

At the end of the third day the shed was finished. We stood to one side and looked it over with pride. The southwest wind was whipping up whitecaps in the bay and was blowing through the woodshed as I had planned, working its magic of drying the moisture from the debris within. Some outcroppings of ledge too big for us to break or move still protruded. They were greenstone, the oldest exposed rock in the world, part of the original earth's crust and underlying all the sedimentary and volcanic formations that had come into being during the last four billion years. Those outcrops had age and stability, were not to be moved like glacial erratics. Furthermore, the spaces between them would soon fill up with bark and chips, odds and ends that were not large enough to qualify as firewood.

In one corner opposite the scraggly pine a clump of birch stood very close to the edge of the roof. We had debated what to do, for one of the trees was a sapling four inches in diameter that would have rubbed the overhang. There were five, silvery birches, tall and straight. Only one leaned toward the shed. I could easily have cut it without destroying the looks of the group, but when I considered the fact it had grown for almost twenty years, I had no heart for putting the axe to its butt. Furthermore, I reasoned, birches should grow in threes and fives and sevens, a numerical pattern that some-how seemed right; so we cut a six inch notch out of the edge of the roof just large enough so the tree could grow for many years to come. In time I might have to enlarge the space, but that could wait—and while I waited the birch would give me joy.

The following morning when I came out of the cabin I viewed our work with delight, and what I saw pleased me, for the woodshed looked as though it had always been there. It was old and weathered, actually an extension of the cabin it-self. After breakfast I pounded two big spikes into the near corner post for the double bitted axe, and on another, one for the cross-cut saw. My shed was ready for the first real wood, or so I thought until I remembered there was neither a chop-ping block or a sawbuck. The block must come first. It must be large and steady, for there is nothing worse than one that is too light and does not stand squarely of its own weight. The one of my boyhood had been used so long its top surface was chewed into a hollow by uncounted thousands of blows, its center a fine maze of shredded wood fiber so that a chunk could almost stand by itself without being held. On that same block many chickens had lost their lives; it was stained dark brown, and tiny tufts of feathers adhered to the wood.

Off the end of the point a pine had blown down. The log was almost two feet through at the butt and solid as the day it had fallen. I sawed off the end and rolled it down the shore to the canoe for it was far too heavy to carry. At the landing below the cabin, I unloaded and rolled it up the trail to its final resting place. As a gesture of triumph, I sank the axe deep into its very center with a mighty first blow.

As to the sawbuck, it must be equally sturdy; so I looked around and found several discarded rafter logs of three to four inches in diameter, made two notched crosses, and fastened them so firmly together I could drop a good sized log on them without danger of breaking through. It, too, looked as though it belonged.

The first wood I gathered was aspen that had blown down after an infestation of forest tent caterpillars had defoliated them years ago. There were dozens of logs, most of them punky and wet, but with drying they would burn well in the fireplace. There were also green ones, cut to make room for the cabin, which were sound and hard. Such wood would need kindling that was dry and resinous, so I searched the lake shore and the swamp back of the beach for old cedar logs. Almost impervious to water, cedar, no matter where it lies, is soon ready to burn. I carried the logs I had found to the level spot in front of the sawbuck and added them to the growing pile.

A weathered pine stump down near the shore had roots and a base still sound. I split it there and carried the chunks to the chopping block. The slivers were yellow and impregnated with resin. I picked one out from a curving root and smelled it. It was strong and vital and impervious to decay. Fat wood, settlers called it, like the pine knots I always gathered, full of the stored sunshine of years ago. Such pieces would all but explode on cold mornings, flame like a torch at night, and light up the cabin when the fire was low.

We have forgotten the use of axes and saws, forgotten the joy of doing physical work. How few today know the feel of an axe as it bites into a log, the solid feel of it going into resin, the clean break of a chunk splitting in the cold. How many know how to saw—that one must not ride the saw on its return, only pull. These things have been forgotten along with walking, paddling, and carrying loads. I discovered once again the satisfaction of laying in a supply of wood beyond my immediate needs, a joy that came, I knew, not only from my own experience, but from that of generations of my forebears preparing for the cold and storms of northern Europe. I thought of the women I had seen in foreign countries carrying bundles of faggots to their homes, of Indians in the old days gathering piles of buffalo chips or twisted bunches of grass on the prairies of the west, of the hoarding of oil and fat in the Eskimo country, of the layers of charred woods and ashes in the caves of primitive man and the built-in consciousness that is ours regarding fuel and fire and the realization that any place where campfires are made is home. One has only to use an axe to set in motion reactions and deep responses that go back to pioneer days.

But more than that, the woodshed brought into sharp focus for me a thousand campsites of my own all over the north. Each night no matter where I happened to be, the final task was gathering wood and kindling for the morning, tucking shreds of birchbark, cedar, or little sticks under the canoe, the tarpaulin, or even in my sleeping bag so the warmth would dry them out. Providing for the day to come seemed as natural and provident as looking at the skies before going to sleep and trying to predict what the weather might bring. A year ago, up in the tundra country northwest of Hudson Bay and beside a gale swept narrows where the caribou crossed, were weather-beaten branch ends of a gnarled, dead spruce with splinters of a resin-soaked root to start them off. In the Quetico-Superior during a recent storm, I found what I wanted on the underside of an old pine log, a bit of wood so dry it was almost dusty in spite of the rain. My woodshed kindled memories as well as fires.

As I began to work on a pine stump, I heard the drone of a jet far overhead. Its vapor trail was a thin white string floating in the blue, its point a beetle boring into space. From that height, the tangled waterways and forests were only a gray-green blur. To the young pilot up there, the world was small for he could move faster than the speed of sound.

Then the skies reverberated as the plane broke the sound

barrier. That pilot was conquering space, his frontiers different than man had ever known. Behind his flight was no association with the past. He flew alone, more alone than man had ever been. Gradually the distant roar blended with the soft whisper of the wind in the trees and then it was gone.

The chickadees were calling again and fluttering all around me, searching the ground for the harvest that was there. A pair of nuthatches flew into the ragged old pine top, came down the trunk headfirst investigating all the activity. A pileated woodpecker drilled noisily into a big aspen just behind and wickered as it flew off to another back of the beach.

I swung the axe again and cut into the raw resin of a root. The grain was fine and golden yellow and, because my axe was sharp, its surface gleamed. There was the embodiment of all that was elemental and afforded me, a man of the space age, a tie with the past. That root which once anchored a pine against the gales, held me to the earth.

After the stump was finished, I split a chunk of cedar into fine straight splinters and stacked them neatly inside the shelter. The axe was placed on its two spikes, the saw hung ready for another day. I gathered up an armful of kindling and several solid pieces and carried them to the woodbox beside the fireplace.

CHAPTER 7

THE SWAMP BUCK

IT WAS the last day of deer season and one of those breathless dawns that seem to come only in November. I stood outside my cabin and looked at the stars blazing against their background of blue-black sky. In the east was a hint of rose, not enough to brighten the horizon or dim the stars, merely an assurance that daybreak was near. The birds were stirring and the sounds of their cheeping filtered out of the pines. Along the shore of the lake new ice was forming on the rocks.

A partridge whirred up noisily from its burrow in a drift,

lit in the top of a white birch where it fed on the frozen brown buds. The rolling tattoo of my pileated woodpecker exploring a dead aspen for grubs, reverberated again and again. Never had it seemed quite so loud, never so continuous a roll. The partridge fussed away, holding precariously to the bending, topmost branches. A pair of chickadees fluttered to the feeding tray. It was a quiet that would not last because hunters were on the trails to their watching places.

For days the hills had resounded to the rattle of rifle fire. Never an hour was it still. The kill was heavy, for the breeding season had been good and there was plenty of browse. A fresh snow had covered most of the evidence: blood-spattered trails, spots where deer had been cleaned, and the long, smooth toboggan tracks made by carcasses being dragged to the roads.

The survivors were wary now, had retreated into swamps, balsam, and jackpine thickets. Many were cripples, would stay in hiding until the furor ended. Those with superficial flesh wounds might recover, those shot through would die. The wolves would pick up some of the trails and finish what the hunters began and the cycle would be complete.

The east was brightening now, the stars fading fast. The pileated woodpecker left its tree and wickered loudly as it flew back into the timber. The partridge in the top of the birch had worked its way out to get at the terminal buds until the branch bent down sharply. Back and forth swayed the bird, and once, almost losing its balance, recovered with a furious flapping of wings.

For some time I watched and listened, then grew cold and went back to the cabin. As I reached the stoop a violent burst of rifle fire came from across the lake, five shots as fast as the hunter could reload—then, after a few minutes, one final report. It was still hardly light enough to see, but the last day of season was underway. From every point of the compass now came a staccato barrage. It was as if the initial fusilade had triggered-off the rest.

Though my days of hunting were long past, I knew what that burst of fire meant, a running deer in the half-light of morning, either a final shot as it disappeared or the *coup de grâce*. The firing had come from in back of the islands near a beaver flowage almost two miles away. Not long before, I had been in there following the little creek that emptied its water into the lake, had watched a beaver bring branches of birch and aspen to a huge pile of winter food a few feet from shore and close to its house on the bank. Two birches of a fine clump of three were already down and the last would soon follow.

From the beaver house I had worked my way into a series of swamps and a morass of tangled windfalls, grass, and alders, to where the creek finally emerged as a seepage from a deep hidden pond. On that exploring trip I saw a fine buck. It was late October and I had climbed a ridge to get a view over the islands and to see the panorama of blue and gold. While standing there completely absorbed, the brush cracked and there was the buck, and a big one, working toward me. He moved leisurely along, stopping now and then to paw the leaves and scratch them away from the green and tender shoots underneath. The animal came on; the wind was in my favor, and I barely breathed for I wanted to see how close he would come. His antlers were broader and more palmate than those of ordinary deer, and I counted four points on a side. Nearer and nearer he came, then stopped to mutilate a scrubby clump of hazel. He combed the brush until it was stripped of bark and beaten down, though the antlers were cleaned of velvet long ago. Now their surfaces all but shone in the yellow light of the aspen around it.

A hundred feet, seventy-five, fifty. Suddenly the animal's eyes grew wide with suspicion, his ears swiveled slowly in my direction. The muzzle was black, nostrils distended, the diamond at the base of the throat startling in its whiteness. Then, without warning, the buck tensed, snorted in alarm, and in one beautiful motion cleared a windfall and went off twenty feet at a jump, his flag flying.

This was where the shooting had taken place. Normally a haven from hunters, the flowage, now that it was frozen, no longer offered protection. As I ate my breakfast I felt that I must know and, though I no longer carried a gun, it would seem good to get out in the hills again and cruise as I used to do. I might find my buck and perhaps see others too, but best of all would be to get the feeling of the November woods.

I took the green canoe and paddled across the lake. It was bitterly cold and though the sun was shining, ice froze on my paddle. There was no wind or spray, for which I was thankful, and I pushed the canoe swiftly across the open lake. The narrows were closing and a rock in the center was already sheathed with glistening white. As I coasted past a timbered island, a squirrel chattered at me from an overhanging pine. It was a glorious morning and with the new snow it should not be too difficult to unravel the story of the shooting.

I tried to land in a marshy bay to the right of a stream but it was frozen solid. Three buffleheads sat at the edge of the ice and fluttered off across the bay as the canoe approached. A last remnant of the migration, they would soon be far to the south. When I found I could not land, I paddled toward the mouth and, as I expected, a boat was pulled up there beside the beaver house. A man's track led from it to the ridge. The hunter was alone; he had worked his way along the creek to a high point from which he could look down into the tangle of windfalls and grass of the flowage. I followed carefully, aware that even though two hours had passed, he might be waiting and watching. Not knowing who he was, there was always danger. At last I reached the high point, looked below as he had done and remembered the day a month before when I had gone into the swamp and turned back because of the treacherous holes of muck. Some of the pools had been alive with minnows then, and in places the water ran free. I had seen northern pike in the spring during the spawning and had watched them swim around in water so shallow their dorsal fins stuck out like sails. A pair of mallards flushed that day, a gorgeous greenhead and its mate, and I watched the sun on blue and green and bronze as they climbed into the sky. Each year they chose that nesting site, for in its depths a brood was safe. Mink, weasels, and foxes prowled the edges hunting for mice and rabbits that abounded there, but few ever penetrated the inner recesses of the sanctuary. No wonder the buck had lived beyond his normal span of years.

I found where the hunter had stopped a moment, and for a hundred yards on top of the ridge his tracks went everywhere. First he had shifted to a new spot so he could look into another part of the swamp, then returned to another place overlooking the lake and examined the vantage points on either side, all this in the first light of dawn. Only an old-timer in the area, someone who knew every stick and stone could have moved like that.

At the far end of the rise, commanding a broad vista across an opening, I found empty shells. Three of them had landed against a ledge above the snow. They were bright and shiny as shells always are when carried in a pocket for some time, .30-30s, from a rifle used by most old hunters in the north. His tracks now ran into the valley. After a hundred yards he had stopped and fired again. That was the last. For a long time I did not move. He might be in there with the deer or watching for any movement in the brush. Then very cautiously I followed his trail once more.

In the open I found the first sign of blood, a thin splattering of tiny droplets, almost a spray of bright red crystals against the snow. It was a buck, and a big one. At first the jumps were long, but quickly changed to a walk. Then I found a bigger burst of blood and evidence of a dragging leg. The animal kept going, circled the second swale completely, and finally went in the direction of a little pond almost a mile away.

All afternoon I followed that trail and late in the day saw where the hunter had given up and turned back. The season was over; one lone shot echoed far beyond the ridges, someone firing at a partridge in a tree, or as a signal to a partner that he was on the way. It was still once more, still as it would be for another year.

The next morning I returned to the beaver swamps and took the trail again. It was not long before I came upon the oval, ice-encrusted bed of the wounded buck, one end stained red from the bleeding flank. He had lain there during the night, then had gone on. The bleeding had stopped and the animal was stiffened and limping. Once when crossing a small gully, he had stumbled and fallen, starting the bleeding fresh. He lay there for some time, then walked around a low windfall that normally he could have cleared with ease. His leg was dragging heavily now, making a long mark in the snow. The flank wound may have been deeper than I thought. Perhaps the hip was injured, in which case there was little chance of recovery; but why hadn't he rested, why hadn't he gone back to his old bedding area in the first swamp? Perhaps wolves were moving in.

Far ahead, three ravens wheeled in ever tightening circles over something they had found. Lower and lower dropped the soaring birds until they disappeared among the trees. I knew the answer then. Somewhere over there I would find what I was looking for.

Old hunters have said that when they pursue a quarry for a long time, they begin to feel and think as the animal does, and Indians have told me that sometimes they become a part of the very creatures they seek to kill. The two days I trailed the buck gave me an intimation of what they knew.

A mile or two beyond, while the buck moved in a great uneven circle, I discovered where the wolves had come close. The running was desperate now and the buck crashed brush and windfalls in its attempt to escape, leaving bits of hide and hair beside the trail. Once he had made a stand against a dense clump of balsam but was in no condition to fight. The unequal contest continued to the shore of the pond but the newly formed ice had settled his fate. Out a little way, he had broken partly through and there he lay, around him blood and a confusion of tracks.

That was the end of the long trail and the way it had always been in the wilds. True, the buck was old and beautiful, but had he escaped the wolves he would have died a lingering death or starved with the coming of the cold and deeper snows. I tried the ice but it was not strong enough to bear my weight, so retraced my steps toward the bay where I had left my canoe.

At the opening where the hunter had fired, I decided to follow the buck back into the swamp from which it had come the morning before. The trails in there were deep in moss and criss-crossed by a labyrinth of rabbit runways. A doe had been there too, and on a small dry hummock grown with long grass and hedged in by a tangle of raspberry, I found two ice-encrusted beds.

Back at the promontory above the mouth of the creek, I stopped to look over the lake once more as I had done the morning of the shooting. The long white windfalls still reached frozen fingers into the shallows and the mottled gray and green of the bush-covered slopes had not changed, but somehow I had changed and within me was a sense of loss. True, this was the way it should be, but my logic was of no help. All I seemed to remember was the beauty of an October day when those shores were blue and gold and how proudly that buck had cleared the windfall and bounded down the slope.

A metallic chuck-chuck came from one of the cabins to the east—someone was splitting wood. I paddled over there on my way back to pass the time of day.

"What luck?" I asked.

"Wounded a big one back in the beaver slough," my friend replied, "Been tryin' to get him for years, but always something happens. Hit him hard too, but couldn't catch up, followed 'til dark and quit. Wasn't bleedin' much, so figgered there was no use tryin' to find his trail again."

I told him then what I had done, how I had followed the buck just to see what happened and finally found where the wolves had dragged him down on the ice.

"Those critters," he muttered, "we'd have a lot more deer if they was all killed off. They kill a deer every few days and sometimes just for fun. They're the ones that make hunting tougher and tougher in this country."

I did not argue for I knew the attitude of many hunters regarding predators, but I could have told him about ecological balances and how wolves and deer, moose and caribou had lived together for centuries in the north; that what determined survival was not predation but the amount of winter food available; that during winters of extreme cold and heavy snow, ten to twenty per cent of the deer herd might die of starvation; that the wolves had actually done the race a favor by eliminating an aged and crippled sire and that the doe, who no doubt was bred, would replace it in the spring.

Not until mid-January did I ski across the lake to the mouth of the creek and the beaver flowage. I felt I must go into the little pond once more.

The beaver house was a smooth white mound now and the brush from the storage pile completely covered. Deer signs were everywhere again, and in the depths of the swamp, where they had gone for protection and food, I counted the tracks of five. The trails were deep, the animals yarded up as they always do when the snow is deep, and feeding heavily on striped maple and dogwood; even balsam, spruce, and tamarack were eaten; and the few cedars, which they preferred, browsed as high as they could reach. If the winter continued as it had begun, only the strong would survive until spring.

On the pond the bones of the buck had been picked clean by wolves, ravens, and foxes. Even weasels and a mink had come out to the unexpected windfall of food. While I was there a whiskey jack flew from the shore and lit on one of the golden tines of the antlers. The bird warbled softly and waited while I took a sandwich out of my pocket.

A soft almost ventriloquial note emerged from its throat and its black eyes were on the bit of food.

I tossed out a piece of bread. The bird caught it swiftly and flew back to the fringe of spruces from which it had come.

CHAPTER 8

THE SAUNA

THE HISTORY of the Finnish steam bath, or *sauna*, goes back well over a thousand years and possibly more. It is even believed that the sauna was where Vikings took their ease, and was what they dreamed of when on raiding expeditions far from home. While the Halls of Valhalla waited in the great beyond for the slain heroes of battle, the saunas with their comforts and delights waited the return of the living. To them its magic never failed and no doubt they played a role in imparting its joys to other peoples. The Mandan Indians of the western plains were using such baths when explorers first found them, and it is thought by some that they may have been influenced by blond Norsemen who penetrated the continent before Columbus.

Its use is ancient, possibly discovered first by prehistoric men who basked in the live steam coming from some volcanic fumarole. Whatever its origin, the principle is the same everywhere, vapor generated by throwing cold water on heated stones. There are as many variations in method and ritual as the people who have learned to enjoy it. In Finland, however, it reached its highest refinement, became so closely allied with tradition and culture that it is inconceivable to think of this hardy race without it.

According to early records, saunas were originally only excavations in the earth, built into the sides of hills, and served both as baths and family dwellings. Later, they were cabins built on flat land with a living room attached; finally, saunas became separate buildings near the water.

In the sauna's mellow, cozy warmth, many a tale was told and many a song sung during the long black winter nights of the north. It was here the legends of *Kalevala* were told and handed down from generation to generation.

The sauna was considered a protection from all troubles, physical as well as of the mind, and it is not without reason the Finnish people say, "If spirits, a sauna, and tar do not effect a cure, then a disease is fatal." In the days of the dark past when demons and spirits were abroad, the Mistress of Pohjala cast an evil spell on all people, bringing pestilence, until it was feared all must die. Vänämöinen, the ancient bard and seer, healed them with the sauna and his incantations. Ever since, the steam bath has been held in reverence and to this day no one within its sacred walls must speak or think of evil.

All over the north of Europe, in the Baltic States as well as in Scandinavia and Finland, the sauna is spoken of with affection and delight. Its use has been so closely woven into the fabric of these cultures, it can never be forgotten even by the most sophisticated. Finnish emigrants brought the custom to America as early as 1683—and it was said that a settler built his bath house first, then his house and barn. In America today, as in Finland, every Finnish farm has its sauna; even in towns and cities one finds them built into homes, or, if this is impossible, into public baths, so important has it become to the way of life of these people. Some are elaborate now, have lost their simplicity in chrome and steel and glass, but the spirit lives on and still invokes its magic, bringing rest and peace to weary bodies and souls.

My sauna cabin is primitive, one step removed from the first excavations in the hillsides of Finland. I wanted it that way for I felt it must be close to the earth, so much a part of the natural environment that simple values would not be lost. Nestled in a grove of cedars back of the beach, its logs are hand-hewn, carefully notched, and weathered a silver gray. The cabin is small, only ten by ten, but a stoop faces the bay which gives it depth and view. In the old days the roof would have had a hole for the smoke to escape, but now a stove pipe leads through it. Handmade benches are around three sides, and there are wooden pegs for towels and clothes. A window is under the peak of the roof and another looks into the birches. Beyond this there is nothing. Simplicity is the keynote, but when steam rises from the stones and the sprays of cedar give off their fragrance, the sauna comes into its own.

Tall aspen stand among the cedars surrounding the cabin, and as the wind blows they whisper an ancient song. Along the ridge protecting it from the north, are birches growing among the rocks, clusters of striped maple, and hazel. Chickadees and nuthatches are around my sauna cabin, and in one of the tallest trees, pileated woodpeckers have built their nest.

A flying squirrel lives in a hole under the roof and, when it comes out, it spreads its legs and sails to the nearest balsam. I saw it the other night and its eyes were liquid and black, its fur a greyish tan and softer than chinchilla, its wing strips edged with sable. A beautiful creature, I am glad it has taken its abode in so important a place as my sauna.

Along the trail to the lake are huge stones with depressions between them reaching down to the dark, wet roots of the cedar. The boulders are covered with sphagnum and in it grow gold thread, violets, and strange fantastic fungi. All these living things are part of the sauna cabin, as they are part of the woods and rocks around it. It is a place of delight and beauty woven into the experience itself.

In the old tradition and as a mark of hospitality, it is the custom to invite a guest to partake of a sauna with you, but only if the guest is willing and deserves the honor. So when my son came home after several years in Libya and Lebanon and full of the things he had seen and done, there was no question of what to do first. It was an afternoon in September that we started the fire in the barrel stove. The water was cold, the ash trees along the shore were turning yellow, the maples beginning to flame. Only the finest spruce was to be burned that day, for this was a great event for us both. Two cedar switches were prepared. We picked them carefully, only the softest and finest from the lower branches of a tree that grew close to the water. The cabin was swept and clean, and a hand-woven rag rug of many colors was laid out smoothly for our feet. Buckets were filled from the lake, two placed on the rocks above the stove, two on the bench before it.

As preparation, we spent several hours at the woodpile, hauling logs of birch, aspen, spruce, sawing them into proper lengths, splitting them to size, and piling them neatly. While we labored with axe and saw, the smoke curled high above us, the rocks became hotter and hotter until they hissed and spat when water was sprinkled on them.

Toward evening all was in readiness. We opened the door and the bathhouse smelled as it should, rich with the pungence of burning, the odors of hot logs and of many saunas of the past. We stripped and took our places on the lower bench.

A dipperful of water tossed onto the rocks all but exploded, instantly filling the cabin with steam. Then more water, again and again, until the steam began to penetrate our bodies. When we had become accustomed to the heat, we moved to the upper bench where it was more intense. As we sat there, we became one with the rising vapors and the crackling spruce in the stove.

"Dip your cedar switch," I said, "dip it in your bucket and sprinkle the stones."

Bob did so, and the air was full of fragrance.

"Hold it to your face," I told him, "hold it close and breathe deeply."

The oil of cedar went into the passageways of our lungs, scoured and renovated them until they were clean and fresh. The moist warmth caressed us and filled us with a lassitude that dispelled all thoughts, and had we not been faithful to the ritual, we might have been tempted to stay and miss one of the greatest thrills of the sauna, the exhilarating plunge into the cold waters of the lake. Watching Bob, and knowing myself, I felt we could wait no longer. The time had come.

"Let's go," I said.

Heated through and through, we dashed down the trail, splashed into the bay, swam furiously for a moment, then returned. How good to feel the warm steam again, and now the perspiration literally rolled off our bodies until we shone and gleamed in the firelight.

"The stones," Bob asked, "where did they come from?"

"The old gravel pit," I answered, "the big ones are on the bottom, smaller ones on top. Notice they are all smooth and dark and of a size, small enough to give maximum surface but not so small they'll cool."

"Polished in some glacial river," he said "and now they're here where they belong."

"Turn your back," I ordered, and I whipped him with the cedar switch until his skin was red and covered with the flat green tips of the branch ends.

He did the same for me and we laughed with the good feeling that was ours of cleanliness, of warmth and blended smells. No ordinary bath could equal this. The pores themselves were cleaned, the blood brought into circulation by the plunge, the entire system recharged, stimulated, and relaxed.

"This is it," said Bob, "elemental; we need nothing more. I had forgotten how good a sauna really could be."

He held the cedar against his face, breathed deeply once more.

"The smell of cedar," I reminded him, "is an incense that carries thoughts to heaven, which is why all worries leave."

"And all evil," he replied, "all intrigue and ambition."

I threw on another dipperful. White steam surrounded us and swirled along the ridgepole.

"About ready," announced Bob, and once more we ran to the beach, this time swam far out for the water was like silk to us, and we did not feel the cold, were conscious only of floating without effort and drifting in a medium as warm as our own bodies.

We went back to a third and last steaming and, when we

returned to the lake for a final dip, the sun was tinting the water, the west was pink and blue, with a broad band of color in the bay. We swam through it and then into the band, lay there in its iridescence, looking toward the sauna in the cedars. Smoke still rose from the chimney, though the fire was almost gone, and we could even smell it there on the water.

After we had cooled, we swam to the beach, went up the trail again, opened the door and windows wide, and dried ourselves leisurely. It was almost dark now and we sat on the lower bench before the open door of the stove and toasted our feet in the glow of the coals. The hot steam was gone and the cool night air felt good to us. The coffee pot was hot and we took it outside, sat on the stoop and drank cup after cup.

"Mead of the Vikings," said Bob.

The horizon was a dull glow against the dark of the ridges. A sudden breeze fluttered the aspen leaves far above, and we could hear the soft rushing of the river at the outlet a mile away. Loons called time and again, first the wild laughing calls, then a last long mournful note.

There was nothing of great moment to talk about, but within us was a feeling of well-being in which the affairs of the world seemed far away and unimportant. Ours was a sense of fullness and belonging to a past of simple ways. After a time we went in and dressed by the firelight. Before going up to the big cabin for supper we stood outside for a while. A sliver of a new moon hung low in the southwest and we could see the outline of the old. Far out on the lake, I heard a flock of mallards. Not long now and great Vs of them would be winging toward the south. Stars were beginning to show and Venus hung like a great lamp in the darkening sky.

This was the time of magic when the world was still, this the feel of dawns and of awakenings at night, of hush and quiet. Life was simple and complete.

CHAPTER 9

THE FEEL OF SPRING

Spring canoe trips into the hinterlands are always exciting adventures after a winter in the north, for impressions then seem as fresh as the country itself. One that stands out boldly from the many I have made over the years is a trip young Sig and I took during the war, when he was at home on a last furlough before going overseas with the 10th Mountain Division. I wanted him to carry something special away with him, something he would remember when the going got tough, the feel of spring and the joy of wilderness travel after the breakup.

It was in May after the ice went out; the sun was shining as though to make up for lost time and the air was full of the smells of thawing earth, open water and swelling buds. The shores of southern slopes were nile green where the aspen stood. Ice crystals sparkled on sedges nearby, and in sheltered bays snowbanks still gleamed. The tinkle of melting ice was everywhere. Ducks whispered overhead and sea gulls wheeled in arcs of silver in the morning light.

"Mountain air," said Sig, "this is the way it feels above timber line."

We stepped into the canoe and pushed off, happy to be paddling again, were going into some back country forgotten by everyone except the loons and explorers such as we. Little lakes, creeks, and beaver flowages off the beaten routes beckoned irresistibly. Seldom seen or used, they were new as the spring was new. The canoe was pointed to the northeast, a chain of boggy waterways south of Knife on the Minnesota-Ontario border. My old friend Jean had told me about them when he heard Sig was coming home, and urged me to take him there to try for trout in one of the clear water lakes.

"No big ones," he said, "but they're mighty pretty, sort of a golden, speckled brown with reddish tips to their fins, and rose underneath."

Jean was an outlaw according to the wardens, and one of the finest woodsmen in the north, and what he knew about the maze of waterways in his domain was nobody's business but his own. Like all frontiersmen, he felt the country belonged to him, was his to use, that trapping was a game and regulations were for outsiders.

"No hard feelings," he told me once, "those game wardens have to make a living, too, and it's their job to keep us out of the beaver country."

The country Jean traveled had always appealed to us, no matter how hard to reach, and going in was a challenge we accepted with delight. Portages were usually overgrown and hard to find, for they did not warrant the time and cost for rangers to keep them open. Beaver sloughs, tiny creeks crisscrossed with windfalls and with barely enough water to float a canoe, strings of little ponds between them, this was the kind of terrain he used.

As we paddled up Moose Lake, it seemed as though we were seeing it for the first time. Spring trips are always that way and the old familiar route we were following to the beaver country was almost strange. Spring, in addition to many other things, is a time for renewal of memories that may have grown dim during the winter, so when we reached a point on Newfound Lake where Camp 25 used to be, I lingered.

It didn't mean much to Sig, but it did to me. The cabin was gone now. Once it had served as a stopping place for rangers, trappers, and lone travelers. Now it was down except for a few foundation logs covered with long brown grass and brambles. A bear had torn one of the logs apart for grubs, and a deer had pawed the earth to get at the salt where the stove had been. I wandered around, remembering bitter winter nights with the stars blazing and the mercury below zero, snowshoe trails leading in, long icicles from the eaves, wolves and foxes hanging from a pole—the winter I made the rounds of the poison trail.

I could see again the yellow light of the window from the last bend in the trail, sniff the wood smoke and then, when the door opened wide, the warm smell of cooking, balsam boughs, the drying outfit. How bright that lantern used to be, how warm and friendly the cabin after a day in the bush. Everything was gone now with Bill and Jack and Gay and the rest—just a grass-grown mound of crumbling logs.

Sig brought me to with a start, "Let's go Dad," he said, "we've quite a stretch to make before dark."

We left Camp 25 and passed into a narrows where deer crossed the ice during the winter and often broke through. Once, seven carcasses lay there frozen in the ice, food for wolves, foxes, and ravens. Somehow they never learned, kept coming winter after winter, though the dead lay plainly in sight. Their trail was an old one and near the water's edge was bare gravel. We went in close, looked down to the bottom, and there in the mud were greenish white bones.

Just beyond we surprised a beaver sunning itself on a rock. It blinked lazily, watched us wide-eyed, slid off and slapped its tail. The channel led into a bay and at its end we could hear the Ensign River rapids. We headed for the sound, fought the current and landed on a grassy bank—the beginning of our first portage. It felt good to stretch our legs and feel the rocks under our feet. The river was high and boiling. Fish were coming up to spawn, suckers, northern pike, walleyes, their black shadows holding steady in the flow.

Ensign was calm, its shores as misty green as those on Moose. A partridge drummed, a muffled hidden beat, steady and slow at first, then a swift crescendo and, when it was over, the sunshine and quiet were even more intense than before. Halfway down the lake we stopped on a flat rocky spit to boil a pot of tea.

"Portage out of the northeast end," said Sig, studying the map, "two or three potholes and flowages and we're on our own."

We spent an hour soaking up the feel of the country, basking in the sun. The whiskey jacks found us swiftly and we fed them bits of bread and meat. A squirrel came down a jackpine and scolded us roundly. Ravens soared, watching the ground below. They knew the best places, the narrows where the deer broke through, the currents between the islands. Nothing ever escaped them. Ours was a sense of golden leisure that comes only in the spring, after months of greyness and cold.

At the end of the lake was a slow, flowing creek separated from the open water by a sand bar. It moved through a swamp grown thickly with sedges, cattails, and alder. A flock of mallards took off from the rushes and the sun glinted on green and bronze as they climbed.

Below the last riffle, we landed and looked for fish but saw none. The portage was low and soggy, and lush buds of marsh marigold showed greenish yellow against the mud. Finding no evidence of a trail, we threw on the packs and canoe and simply followed the bank of the creek. Going up a birch-grown slope we jumped a doe and a fawn, and a little farther on found a beaver pond with a house in its center. We dropped the canoe, pushed into the flowage and paddled between great silvery boles of tamarack and spruce. Redwings sat on every cattail and shrub, the males flaunting their crimson epaulets and pouring their hearts out in song. It was as though all the blackbirds in the north had congregated there that day to make us glad—and never for a moment were they still. This was a sound that comes only in May, when their singing is a warbling symphony to spring.

After the flowage, we portaged through alders and a tangle of willow until we found another widening where we poled the canoe with our paddles and pulled it forward by holding on to the brush. All the time we were heading east.

"This is Jean's country, all right," said Sig, "exactly the sort of a layout he'd like."

At the far end of the valley we heard running water and went over to investigate. This was different from what we had seen; it was clear, and foaming white where it dropped over a ledge. A school of suckers lay with noses into the flow. We watched as they threw themselves over the rocks onto the ledge, to rest for a moment on their sides, then with a convulsive effort reached the pool above.

Sig reached down from the bow, slipped his hand into the gills of one of them, held it up for me to see. The fish squirmed powerfully and it was all he could do to keep his grip. Black on top, white with a rosy tint underneath, had it not been for the mouth, it might have been beautiful.

"How about supper?" he said, "this time of year they're good."

"I'm not proud," I answered, "but let's wait, we're not starving yet."

He lowered the sucker gently into the boiling current and released it. For a while it was quiet, gills opening and closing, then with a lunge was back in deep water again.

As we lifted the canoe onto the bank, the brush crashed and we glimpsed a black shadow heading up the creek. Portaging, we found several half-eaten fish the bear had been gorging on as all bears do along the spawning streams of the north. We did not see it again, but heard it beside the creek; it did not want to leave its feeding.

After several portages we finally came onto the shore of a narrow lake about a mile in length. The slopes were rocky and covered with jackpine and spruce, and a spit of a point lay invitingly to one side. A loon called in greeting and the water sparkled in the sun.

"This is it," said Sig, "here's the lake Jean told you about."

We were alone, with all the time we needed to explore its reefs and shallows, to find where the trout had spawned the fall before. There was no sign of a camp, no tent poles, or a fireplace, nor marks of any kind. The site was virgin and unused. I didn't expect to find Jean's setup in the open for, like all outlaws, he stayed back in the bush, left no telltale trails or axe marks that might give him away. He moved through his domain like an Indian, traveled only at night.

"Come here," said Sig excitedly, "I've found something."

I went over to him and there beneath a gray, protruding ledge, hidden with moss and pine needles, he had found five rusty beaver traps.

"Here is the proof," he said, "this is his country."

He placed the traps back carefully under the ledge and covered them with moss.

The sun was down now, the lake beginning to glow. We built a fireplace out of the greenish-gray slabs of slate near the water's edge, pitched the tent as close to the fire as we dared, with a view down the lake. We could watch the fire before going to sleep, and would waken with a vista before us. Such things were important to us, though of course there was the hazard of a gale blowing sparks from the fire, or even of snow and rain, but those we were willing to face.

After supper the dusk settled quickly and the loons called as they always do south of Knife: long, rolling peals of laughter from every point of the compass, merging at last into a weird, continuous harmony that somehow epitomizes the spring breakup better than any other sound. There was magic in the air and in the morning we would know if what Jean had said was true. It was good to lie there in our bags watching the glow of our dying fire and the deeper glow of sunset beyond; but most of all it was good to feel the ground again and to know we were back in a country we loved.

The day dawned clear and as the sun burst over the ridges to the east we were bathed in its warmth. We cooked breakfast, assembled our gear, picked out flies and spinners on a chance the trout would be near shore. Anything could happen, there might be no reefs, the fish already deep. We followed the north side, casting the shallows all the way, but not a strike did we get.

"Might be too early," I said, "sometimes they don't hit for several weeks after the ice goes out."

I wanted so desperately to get some trout for Sig's sake, but try as we might, nothing took hold. At the very end of the lake was a rocky peninsula, almost an island, with a shallow gravel reef between it and the shore. If ever there was a spot, this was it. If the trout had spawned there in the fall, they must still be close—but each time we drifted through it was the same.

We changed lures and went deeper, but all we caught were snags. By midafternoon a wind came up out of the east, clouds covered the sun, and it grew cold. We landed on the rock beside the reef and built a big fire out of windfalls. The gale increased and suddenly there was a drift of snow in the air. Once more we tried the shallows with the same result, then paddled back to camp without a word.

We tightened the tent ropes, cut a good supply of wood, got ready for the storm. The chickadees stopped their singing, squirrels and whiskey jacks disappeared, and by the time we crawled into our sleeping bags the ground was white. For a long time we lay watching the flames, and went to sleep with the sound of snow and sleet hissing into the coals and whispering against the frozen tent.

Spring in the north is strange and wonderful and always full of change. We thought of the long paddle back, the slippery portages with an icy wind over the open reaches toward home.

"The sun will be out tomorrow," said Sig, "it's got to come out."

"It will," I replied, but I knew better with the blow coming out of the east.

Several inches of snow fell during the night and in the morning it looked like November. The water was leaden, the new green of the aspen-covered slopes now a bank of white. It was bitterly cold, the wind high, so we built up the fire and I made a breakfast for explorers who needed strength and courage to face the day: porridge, bacon, eggs, bread, and plenty of hot coffee. As we basked in the warmth our spirits rose and we both had the same idea.

"Listen, Dad," said Sig, "there were a lot of dry logs on

that rock. We could paddle over there, get a real blaze going, dash out to the narrows, fish for a while and come back to get warm."

"Besides," I told him excitedly, "this change of weather might just start the trout feeding. Sometimes this is all it takes."

We put on all the clothes we had, fought the waves to the ledge, and in a short time had a roaring fire underway. When we were thoroughly warmed again we pushed the canoe into the narrows and over the reef we had tried the day before.

Sig's first cast brought a strike and a good one, and I watched him land that fish as though I had never seen it done before. This would tell the story. The trout fought hard, raced under the canoe, went down and surfaced once. Tiring, it came close. I reached down and lifted it into the canoe. A beauty it was, golden brown with reddish fins, a decided blush of color along the sides. We hooted with joy and laughed as the snow swirled around us. By that time we were both so numb we were forced to return. Another log, and the blaze went high. We slapped our hands together, pummelled each other roundly, and soaked up the heat until we were ready once more.

This time it was my turn and in a moment I had one as beautiful as the first—only a couple of pounds, but as hard, firm, and well-colored as any trout I'd seen. Again we sped back to get warm.

The next time we both fished, hooked two trout at once

and got our lines so hopelessly snarled it took an hour to get them untangled. By noon we had all the law allowed, paddled back to camp happy as two *voyageurs* could ever be. We had found our little lake and the trout Jean had told us about. What is more, we had caught them in a howling snowstorm on flies and spinners.

That night we celebrated and each of us had a fish for supper, knowing they would never taste so good again. Trout fried a golden brown, hush puppies in the fat, a can of beans and tea. We piled logs on the fire and crawled contentedly into our bags. The storm could howl now and we didn't care. Tomorrow was another day.

In the morning we took down the frozen tent, packed the outfit and started down the creek the way we had come, slipping and sliding over rocks and windfalls, snow whipping our faces from the brush. A smooth, rocky slope we had come over easily was treacherous now and once I fell with the canoe. Another time we crossed a rocky stream bed, its boulders covered with a smooth, unbroken blanket of white. Each step was a gamble, a chance for a broken leg or a sprained ankle.

But paddling was the worst, with gusts of snow and spray freezing onto our clothes, until it was hard to bend our arms. Mitts were of no use and our frostbitten hands took a beating. At each portage we stopped to build a fire and several times debated whether to go on or to pitch camp until the storm had blown itself out. Only one hitch to that, Sig was soon due at Camp Hale and the end of his furlough was near, so we abandoned any thought of giving in, fought our way down mile by frozen mile, past Camp 25, down Newfound and the full sweep of Moose.

By late afternoon we were at the landing at the south end of the lake where our cruise had begun four days before. We unloaded, went back to the water and stood looking down the lake. White flecked combers and blowing drift were out there. Then the sun burst through a rift in the gray, scudding clouds and for a glorious instant the waters were blue again and the shores dazzling with silver and nile green. We looked at each other and laughed. We had won, found what we had gone in for—the feel of spring—and had some trout as proof. We had known the thrill of exploring forgotten country together, and had seen it at its best.

CHAPTER 10

WILD RICE

WHEN I LOOK at my bag of wild rice, I feel rich. Food of the north, this is nature's wheat, the traditional staple of Indians in the lake states. True, they have many other foods, but this wild grain, gathered in the shallow, mud-bottomed lakes and rivers of the north Middle West, is more important to them than any other. Bloody tribal wars were once fought for its possession, and those whose lands included stands of it were considered wealthy and insured against starvation and want.

Wild rice is easy to prepare; it needs only to be washed, to have boiling water poured over it and be allowed to steam to make it palatable. It should never be boiled, for that may result in a gray, gluey mass, unless mixed with meat or fat. As a stuffing for wild ducks, as a side dish, or cooked with game or fish, it is superb. Even for breakfast with berries, cream, and sugar, it could give modern cereals severe competition. It can even be popped like corn in a skillet, or mixed with bacon, mushrooms, or cheese; wild rice can be served as an entire meal or in infinite combinations with other foods. A purely American dish, it is indigenous to the north.

"Give me five hundred pounds of rice," said my friend Henry Chosa, "and I can feed my family for a year. A few fish now and then, some snared rabbits, a bear and some venison, and there's nothing to worry about. Rice, bear fat, and fish, are all an Indian needs to keep him strong and healthy."

When the fur trade began some three hundred years ago, it did not take the *voyageurs* long to discover the virtues of wild rice, and soon after it was used for barter. They looked forward to it after their monotonous diet of parched corn, pea soup, and salt pork, and eagerly awaited the time when their canoes entered the rice country of northern Wisconsin, Minnesota, Michigan, and southern Ontario where it thrived. While wild rice never attained the prominence of that western plains mixture of dried buffalo meat and tallow known as pemmican, it nevertheless contributed greatly to exploration and trade.

Father Marquette, on his expedition with Joliet in 1673,

spoke of the tall grass growing in small rivers and swampy places which "The Savages Gather and prepare for food in the month of September." He told how they shook the ears from the hollow stems into their canoes, dried them on a grating over a slow fire, and trod the grain to separate the straw.

Radisson, in the journal of his expedition into this area in 1660, left this account:

"Our songs being finished, we began our teeth to work. We Had a kind of rice much like oats. It grows in the water three or four feet deep. They have a particular way to gather up that grain. Two take a boat and two sticks, by which they get the ear down and get the grain out of it. Their boat being full, they bring it to a fit place and dry it, and this is their food for the most part of the winter, and they do dress it thus: for each man a handful of that they put in the pot, that swells so much that it can suffice a man."

Many explorers and traders spoke of wild rice as excellent and tasty food. Alexander Henry, stated in 1775, "The voyage could not have been prosecuted to its completion" without the supply of wild rice acquired from the Indians at Lake of the Woods, and Daniel Harmon mentioned in 1804 that each year, they bought from 1200 to 1500 bushels.

The French called the plant, known scientifically as *Zizania aquatica*, *folle avoine* meaning wild or foolish oats, and from this came the name of a Wisconsin tribe of rice gatherers. Early records always speak of them as the "Folles Avoines," though their real name was Menominee, coming from *Omanomen*, meaning rice, and *Inini*, person—people of the rice. The name Wisconsin may also have stemmed from association with the grain—*Weese-coh-seh*—meaning a good place in which to live, the good place may well have meant where wild rice grows and game and fish are plentiful.

When I see my bag of rice, I think of many things, for it holds far more than food. In addition to high nutrient value and flavor, it has certain intangible ingredients that have to do with memories, and for those who know the country where it grows and have taken part in the harvesting, it has powerful nostalgic associations that contribute as much to the welfare of the spirit as to the body.

There are many legends and stories about how wild rice came to the Indian people, but this is the one I like best. In the days of long ago, it was the custom for the chief to send young boys approaching manhood into the woods to live alone and prove their strength and courage. They existed on berries, roots, and anything they could find, and were told to stay out many days. Sometimes they wandered very far, got lost, and did not return. During these long and lonely journeys, spirits spoke to them and they had dreams and visions from which they often chose a name. If they returned, they became hunters and warriors, and in time took their places in the councils of the tribe.

One year a young boy wandered farther from the village than all the rest. It was a bad time for berries and fruits and he was sick from eating the wrong kinds. This boy loved all that was beautiful and, though hungry, always looked about him for flowers and lovely plants. One night in a dream, he saw some tall, feathery grass growing in a river. More beautiful than any he had ever seen, it changed color in the wind like the waves on a lake. Upon awakening he went to the river and there was the grass, tall and shining in the sunlight. Though starved and weak, he was so impressed that he waded into the river, pulled some plants from the mud, wrapped their roots in moss and bark, and started at once toward the village.

After many days he saw the tepees before him and when at last he showed what he had found, his people were happy and planted the still wet roots in a little lake nearby where it grew for several years until it became a field of waving grass in the bay. One fall a wise old Indian, who had traveled in many countries and knew all things, came to visit the village. He was taken to the lake to see the beautiful tall grass one of their young men had found. Seeing it, he was amazed, raised his arms high and cried in a loud voice:

"Manomen—Manomen—a gift from the Manito."

He explained that the seeds were good to eat, showed them how to gather it and separate the chaff from the grain. Before he left, he advised them to plant it everywhere, guard it well, and use it forever. The Indians have never forgotten—and now all over the north country it grows in golden fields.

In the old days each family had a portion of a rice field as its own, outlined by stakes and established as a claim long before the rice was ripe. Sometimes as an aid in harvesting, and to protect the grain from the ever present threat of being blown off by the wind, the Indians tied it into small sheaves. Basswood fiber was used, one length fastened to another until a large ball was made. The ball was placed on a birchbark tray behind the woman doing the tying, one end of the fiber going over her shoulder through a birchbark loop to her hand. As the canoe was pushed through the rice, she gathered it in with a hoop and with a deft motion tied it together. The rows were long, their straightness a matter of pride. Now the rice was claimed, and safe from the storms.

At harvesting time, a camp was set up on the shore of a lake or river where wild rice grew; often several families banded together. Equipment was simple: canoes propelled by long, forked poles, rice-beating sticks, birchbark, woven matting of cedar, canvas, kettles or tubs for parching, trays for the winnowing, bags or bark containers for storage.

Few food supplies were taken along on these expeditions, the natives depending almost entirely on rice with fish, game, and berries; maple sugar from the spring gathering was often the only seasoning. At night the women set their nets and in the morning drew them out. If fishing were good, drying and smoking racks were set up and fires kept going constantly. The men hunted the fat, rice-fed ducks, shot moose, bear, or deer wherever they could find them. Snares were set for rabbits and partridge, blueberries were picked and dried, a great supply of food laid by for the all important days when harvesting took all their time.

Each day after work around camp was done, they started for the rice fields, usually not to return until midafternoon. A canoe full of rice was considered a day's harvest if there were any distance to go, but if the field were close, several loads could be picked in a day.

Warm, still days were ideal for harvesting, as winds and rain could ruin an entire crop within an hour, a catastrophe not unknown. This was the reason for tying the heads, for then the storms could come without danger of losing all. Not all the rice was picked; some was left for seed and some for the ducks, who were not only good to eat, but planted the rice, as they believed, in many places.

In small camps the parching and threshing was done in the afternoon and evening, and those who did the harvesting assisted; but in large camps where several families worked together, this all important activity was carried on by trusted experts who did nothing else.

Some years ago, in early September, I carried my canoe across the Basswood portage to Hula Lake where I knew the Indians were camped. Long before I reached the tents and tepees along the shore, I could smell the rich pungence of the parching fires, for their haze hung over the woods and blended with that of fall. Just before I reached the camp I stopped and rested my canoe in the crotch of a tree. A dog barked—someone was chopping—and then I heard what I was listening for, the modulated voices of Chippewas talking. It was a pleasant sound, rising and falling, an obligato to the rustling of leaves and to the lazy smoke drifting through the trees, part of the hush which seems to lie over the rice beds before they turn to gold.

Continuing the portage, I walked through the camp, dropped my canoe at the landing and returned. The men were sitting around resting and smoking after their day in the rice fields, women tended parching kettles, some tossed winnowing trays in an open place. Over a central fire was a tripod of white birch poles and from it hung a great iron kettle. An old woman was stirring and the fragrance of a wild rice stew made me hungry for the evening meal. Just beyond, another woman was chopping wood. Dogs and children ran happily about. Some canoes were still out, others returning loaded to the gunwales with green rice.

The field lay greenish gold in the light and the aspen where the camp was pitched took up the color, deepened and spread it all over the shore. Flocks of ducks were over the rice with a constant movement and flashing of wings; they paid little attention to the harvesters. Mostly black ducks, they were heavy and sluggish with the rice they had been gorging. When canoes came close, the ducks rose reluctantly to alight a short distance away, only to hurdle the canoes on their flight back. The harvest of succulent water-soaked kernels on the bottom was also theirs. Already fat as butter, they had a flavor no other fowl could equal.

David Thompson, a famous explorer in the late seventeen hundreds, spoke not only of the rice but of the ducks, stating in his diary:

"Mr. Sayer and his Men passed the whole winter on wild rice and maple sugar, which keeps them alive, but poor in flesh. It was a weak food, those who live for months on it enjoy good health, are moderately active, but very poor in flesh."

However, when he wrote about the ever present ducks, he was more enthusiastic for he said, they "become very fat and well tasted."

Had he known what the Indians knew, that wild rice must be eaten with fish, game, bear fat, or mixed with berries, to be a complete food, he might have changed his opinion of its nutrient value.

The scene before me had a certain timelessness. Except for the fact that Indians now had iron kettles, canvas, and modern tools, instead of birch-bark canoes, matting, and utensils made of cedar and other woods, it was little different from the age of copper and stone. These people were enjoying themselves. Rice gathering was never work, it was the occasion for a festival, with a sense of good feeling and industry that seemed to permeate the camp, the sea of tall grass out on the lake, and the very air itself.

I paddled out where some of the canoes were still harvesting. Joe and Frances were working down one of their rows, Joe poling the canoe, Frances using her rice sticks to gather in the grain. I sat quietly, watching. What a smooth and even rhythm, first the bending of the stalks to the gunwale, then a stroke with the beating stick, never a waste motion, the action almost hypnotic in its effect. Already there were several inches of the long, green kernels on the bottom. In a short time they would be ready to return.

"Good rice," said Joe without stopping the movement of his pole, "nice big rice and clean."

He leaned down, held up a handful for me to see, let it run between his fingers into the canoe. I paddled close, felt it myself. The kernels were long and heavy, as fine a crop as I had ever seen.

"I save some for you," he said, and that fall it was his bag of rice that hung from my rafter.

Later I followed the canoes back to camp and watched the preparations. First the green rice was spread on canvas in partial shade where the sun would not shine on it directly. Heating and mold could destroy it so it was stirred and dried evenly, a process that took most of a day depending on the weather.

After the first drying, the rice was parched, over a slow fire, in a large kettle or tub placed in a slanting position so it could be stirred by someone sitting beside it. The heat was carefully regulated, but skill was required so the kernels did not burn or scorch. The quantity done at one time was seldom more than a peck and it usually required an hour before it was finished. The woman doing this work felt her responsibility, for a moment's neglect or carelessness could destroy the work of many hours. She wielded her slender stirring paddle with a sense of importance, knowing the contents of her kettle might be the last should a storm or wind blow up before the harvest was finished.

Parching loosened the husks and imparted a smoky flavor to the rice. The paddle went round and round, through the rice and underneath, never still for a moment. A stick at a time was pushed into the fire, no large ones or any that might flame. The heat must be constant and slow.

But there was another and far more ancient process in use that day: green rice placed on a rack lined with marsh grass over a smoldering fire. Slower than the kettle method of parching, it dried the grain as one might dry vegetables, berries, or meat. This was "hard rice," greenish black when finished, requiring longer to cook. Keeping indefinitely, it was stored against emergencies and long trips.

After the rice was thoroughly parched by either process, it was put into a barrel or tub for the pounding which loosened the sharp husks and prepared the grain for treading. A wooden pestle, somewhat pointed at one end, was moved gently up and down near the edge of the mortar, never pushed, but allowed to drop of its own weight. It was considered an art to finish the pounding so most of the rice was whole. Broken and shattered grain was the mark of an amateur. While as good for eating as the other, something was lost in quality and appearance that was a matter of pride to the Chippewas.

The final step in the process was the treading to dislodge the fragments of husk. For this, a wooden receptacle holding about a bushel was partially sunk in the ground. A strong cross-pole was tied between two trees at a height of about four feet directly in front of it. The treading was done by a young man wearing a clean pair of new moccasins especially made for this purpose and tied tightly around the ankles. The sole of the foot, so Indians believe, is particularly adapted to this work, is soft, gentle, and firm in its movements.

I watched a man do this all important work; his treading like that of a dancer, his entire being in action. Leaning on the cross-pole and taking the weight off his feet, his body moved with undulating rhythm and sinuous grace. He felt the rice beneath his feet, massaged it, turned it over, almost caressed it in his attempt to separate the precious kernels from their hard and flinty husks. Before the days of wooden tubs, a hole was dug in the ground and lined with deer skin, but the process was exactly the same, a work of care, devotion, and artistry. Many Indians look with favor on the old ways, feel that to deviate too much from ancient customs means a loss not only in flavor, but in the meaning of the food.

After the treading came the winnowing and for this the threshed rice was carried to an open place where wind could sweep away chaff and hulls. It was either tossed and caught in a tray or poured from a height onto a canvas underneath. If the wind was dry and strong, and if parching, pounding, and treading had been well done, the chaff was all blown away, leaving the greenish, black kernels clean and ready for use.

The finished product was now poured carefully into bags, sewn tightly, and placed under cover. Some was for sale to whites, or for trade with other Indians, but most was saved for winter food. Once birch bark or woven matting was used for containers, but now the bags are of burlap or canvas. Their contents were always precious and guarded well.

One night there was a dance, the rice or harvest dance. Everyone dressed for the occasion and there was much excitement and laughter. Kettles were steaming with new rice, game, and berries. The bags were placed under cover where all could see and admire them, for the harvest was almost over. This was a night to be happy and to thank the Manito for his largesse and for a fine harvest season.

After dark when everyone was fed and the fire built up, the drums began their rhythmic beating and the dancers took their places. At times only men danced in a circle around the fire, sometimes only women, often both, the usual stepping and stomping to the steady beat of the drums. That night after the dancing had gone on for several hours, I saw a young man, possibly more gifted and imaginative than the rest, begin to imitate the actions of the harvest, the motion of poling a canoe through the water, the graceful swinging of the rice sticks, the circular motion of the paddle in the parching, the dance of the treader holding on to his balancing pole, the final winnowing with a tray. Others soon followed the inspired one until there was much confusion, each attempting to interpret some part of the many aspects of harvesting and preparation. Finally, tiring, they relapsed into the ancient broken half-step of all native dances, a ritual looked forward to by all the band.

I have not seen a harvest dance for a long time now, and it is possible younger Indians do not remember, or if they do would think it old-fashioned and beneath their dignity to indulge, but those who have seen and taken part, cannot forget the deep joy and meaning of such celebrations.

In the fall when the rice harvest is on, I think of canoes going through golden fields of it against the blue of the water, the flash of ducks above and the whisper of their wings, the redolent haze from parching fires over some encampment. I remember the drums and the dancers under a big September moon, the soft voices of the Chippewas, the feeling of these Indian harvesters of the lake country for this gift of their Manito, long ago.

CHAPTER 11

THE ROSS LIGHT

YEARS AGO on a canoe trip with photographer Frank Ross of the *Saturday Evening Post,* I learned something about light I did not know before. For a long time I had been aware of the magic of those last slanting rays of the setting sun but, until that memorable trip with him, I was not fully aware of their significance and possibilities. I discovered with him that unusual effects could be achieved during certain rare moments when the light was just right, that color and depth were accentuated to the point where ordinary scenes could become spectacular pictures. Day after day we waited patiently for the time to come, were often disappointed, but when we caught what we were looking for, it was worth all the time and effort.

Sunsets had always brought me joy and I had marveled at those almost level rays before the sun dropped below the horizon, but with him I became so completely conscious of their wonder that never again did I accept them with complacence. I discovered later that even more than the beauty of the sunset itself, or its miraculous color effects, was a certain indefinable impact on the mind that brought a scene within the realm of unreality and gave it a patina it did not have before. In its glow came deeper meaning and dimension and, at the moment, all that was bathed in it was illumined and exalted until the vision before me became one of fantasy and delight.

We were paddling along through the rushes of Moose Bay off the mouth of the Robinson River when I first saw this glowing afternoon light with Ross. The shore was good for game and we watched it closely. Moose and deer often came out there, and once I had seen a bear with two cubs splash across the sand spit that separates the bay from Crooked Lake. A long beach was screened by rushes, and the spruces behind it stood tall and dark. Something moved, and there was a big buck with a splendid set of antlers wading sedately through the shallows.

Frank readied his camera and I pushed forward silently

without taking my paddle from the water. The buck was unaware, but the light was bad against the darkening shore. Then suddenly the sun flashed through a cloud bank and for an instant the antlers were gleaming gold and the entire scene transformed. The animal saw us and in a series of tremendous leaps headed for the bank with golden spray flying all around. The spruces were splashed with it and our minds as well. I turned the canoe and paddled back through the dusk toward camp. We had seen more than the buck, more than the light itself, and neither of us spoke.

Francis Lee Jaques once painted a lone caribou bull on a tundra shore, and there again was the light catching one tip of an antler, turning it to gold. I studied that picture and though the entire scene was magnificent, it was the glint on that single tine which fascinated me. Without that flash of gold, it still was a great painting, but with it the scene was enhanced by something more than beauty; with new meaning and dimension.

Time and again since that trip I have sat in my canoe across from a stand of red pine waiting for the light as Frank and I had done. During the day, trunks have a glint of reddish brown which toward dusk may heighten and turn to deeper red or copper, but when the Ross light strikes, those boles are changed to gleaming gold, and if there are birch or aspen near by, some of their shimmering whiteness may be washed with it until the trees shine with glowing pink. I have seen a curving shore of birch close to a stand of red pine look as though someone had dipped a soft brush in their color and stroked the fringe of an entire bay.

All who have known the mountains have waited for the alpenglow, when snow-clad peaks turn red for just a moment, and glaciers and streamers of ice hang like colored ribbons from the heights. Long after the valleys are dark, those peaks continue to glow, and as the light recedes, they fade to purple and then to black with only the highest pinnacle flaming to the end.

Late one afternoon I stood on the banks of the Yukon River just as the sun was sinking below the horizon. Some ducks took off as the Ross light struck, and they rose from a river that was no longer brown and took with them from its golden surface a cascade of glittering droplets. But it was later when our plane took off that I really saw the light and what it did to the vast Yukon valley, the great flats, the innumerable ponds and estuaries, the unending muskegs, the rims of pointed spruce. All the limitless and unending loneliness was gone and, as I looked down from high above, I was entranced with the warmth and glowing color. Every bit of water had turned to gold and, as the valley darkened, it looked as if molten metal had been spilled and dribbled over the black velvet of the land.

The Ross light does strange and wonderful things to all who see it and are sensitive to its meaning. No two ever see it alike, but this much is true, somewhere within it is a power that transfigures everything, even those who watch.

Anya Seton speaks of this in her book, *The Winthrop Woman*, for in this same light Telaka and Elizabeth forgot their tragedy and were calm. They were sitting in the woods near the shore when the glow covered them. Telaka, the Indian woman, noticed it first and spoke:

"Look," she said, "and be quiet."

"At the touch of the slim brown hand, a thrill ran up Elizabeth's arm. The pool, the rock, the hemlock trees shifted and changed focus. Each one stood out distinct and seemed to shimmer. The wind blew stronger, she heard it whispering and rushing by. A ray of sunlight slanted down between the tree trunks, it touched the pool with liquid gold.

"The pool became transparent to its golden depths, and herself was plunging into those depths and yet upraised with joy upon the rushing wind. The light grew stronger and turned white. In its crystal whiteness there was ecstasy. Against the light, she saw a wren fly by, the wren was made of rhythm, it flew with meaning. There was the same meaning in a caterpillar that inched along the rock, and the moss and the little nuts which had rolled across the leaves.

"And still the apperception grew, and the significance. The significance was bliss. It made a created whole of everything she watched and touched and heard, and the essence of this created whole was love. She felt love pouring from the light, it bathed her with music and with perfume, the love was far off at the source of light and yet it drenched her through. And the source and she were one.

"The minutes passed. The light moved softly down and faded from the pool. The ecstasy diminished, it quietened, but in its stead came a serenity and sureness she had never known.

"Telaka's hand was trembling. Elizabeth looked at the squaw's face and no longer saw the mutilation. She saw it whole and still touched by the afterglow."

One of the most dramatic sights in the north is this light on a field of wild rice. Until the time of the light's coming, the rice may be yellow or even tan against the blue of the water, but when the rays strike it exactly right, the rice may turn to solid gold. I stood in my blind on Back Bay of Basswood Lake in late October. It had been a wild, blustery day with snow swirling constantly. Toward evening the sun broke through the gray clouds and, when it washed the rice beds, the fury was forgotten—the wet and frozen hands, the shivering in the teeth of the wind—and for a moment there was a sense of warmth and quiet in which I was no longer conscious of the storm. Silhouetted against the lowering sky that evening were flights of ducks and in the shaft of light they became drifting skeins, silver as they turned, gold as they flew into the west.

Later, on the shore of Burntside Lake, I watched the new ice forming. Some parts of the bay had already closed, but before me the water was still unfrozen. It was calm, and crystal spears extended over the surface like a net. A deep uneasy rustling came from the expanding ice of the far shore. Before long the bay would be sealed.

As I stood there the sun broke through a mass of dark

clouds and the scene was etched with light. The streaks of open water became iridescent, the forming crystalline spears were like splintered glass in red and silver, the channel a shifting kaleidoscope of rose and vermillion, orange and mother of pearl against the blue. I turned and looked at the border of marsh grass back of the beach and it was solid gold, the brown windrow of pine needles along its edge awash with it. The sun dropped, and all the color was gone, there was only the sound of the whispering ice to remind me of what I had seen.

During the winter while skiing down the Lucky Boy Trail near my home, I stopped where it leads south to an abandoned mine. At the turn stands a clump of tall spruces loaded with clusters of cones. As I rested there, I heard a soft twittering, and looking up saw that the tree tops were alive with pine grosbeaks. Bracts and scales from the seed cones on which they were feeding, floated down in a shower of brown. I could not see the color of the birds in the growing dusk until the sun came out and a shaft of light struck the spruce tops. During that instant the cones became masses of gold and the grosbeaks turned to Chinese red. The birds felt the warmth of that last ray and their warbling and aliveness intensified and filtered down to me, making my resting place part of their glory. The moment passed as swiftly as it had come; the spruce tops turned black, the birds lost their brilliance and then flew back into the woods. I had stopped there many times, but had never before been fortunate enough to arrive while the birds were feeding at sunset.

In February while the river was still partly open, I skied along its banks. The drifts were very deep and great sloping mounds of them lay close to the rapids. Rabbit tracks ran over them and in places partridge had walked. It was a time of bitter cold and the colors there were blue and white, blue for the water and sky, white for the snow and ice—that is, until the Ross light came. Then the open rapids became red as blood, with the snow and ice bleeding into them, the color spreading over the banks until the entire river was covered, and the trees, grasses, and shrubs were black silhouettes against it.

One summer I watched a storm build up over a little lake in the Quetico-Superior. We were camped on an island covered with huge white pines and our vista lay unbroken to the east and up a long bay where the shores were rugged and stark. Tall bulrushes grew in the sand around our end of the island, and the broken stump of a tree lay grotesquely in the water close to the landing.

For an hour great masses of snowy cumulus had boiled and churned and now their summits were tinted with color from the setting sun. Black clouds moved among them, and from their ominous depths lightning flashed and the thunder rolled until it echoed and re-echoed from the shores. It grew darker and darker and the waters were calm.

Over the lake lay a sense of impending doom and we made everything safe: canoes well up among the trees, tent stakes reinforced, ropes so tight they sang when we touched them. All we owned was covered; food, equipment, dry wood under tarpaulins weighted down with heavy stones. We were at the shore ready to fly for the tent the instant the wind and deluge came.

Then a strange and eerie light was over the lake and the surrounding hills, a greenish-yellow glow that was almost tarnished gold. Rushes once black were illumined now, leaned like silver rapiers as the air began to move. The stump became alive, lost its jagged contours, and was a thing of beauty against the opalescence of the water. The cliffs and pines across the channel turned to burnished copper. Then came the wind and the rain in a final crashing rumble—and the glory was gone.

And so it has been ever since my trip with Frank Ross. To me this light has been a constant source of pleasure, and looking for it an adventure. When it comes I feel something unexpected has been my reward, a rich dividend on an investment of hours of waiting and watching.

PAYS D'EN HAUT

PAYS D'EN HAUT

The Upper Country

To THE NORTH *and west of Lake Superior and far into Canada lie thousands of miles of lakes, rivers, forests, and tundra, the land the French voyageurs spoke of as the upper country, the far country, and the land beyond. It reaches as far as the Rocky Mountains to the west and the Hudson Bay region to the northeast. Beyond it lie the barren lands of muskeg, bog, and mountainous hills that border the Arctic Coast and continue on into the great islands of the High North.*

This is a rugged land with powerful brawling rivers and enormous lakes so broad their shores are lost in distance. It is the land of the moose, the caribou, and the wolf. Beyond the tree line, the Arctic fox, the ptarmigan, and the lemming are at home. The Crees live there and the Chipewyans, and such little known tribes as the Dog Ribs, Hares, and Yellow Knives. Above them to the north are the Eskimos.

It is a land of space, solitude, and forbidding grandeur. Gone are the red and white pine, the silvery canoe birch, and the cedar. Horizons are somber with black-pinnacled spruce, or lie stark and naked against the sky. It occupies most of the Canadian Shield and is as hard, unyielding, and bleak as its native granites. Here is no intimacy and familiar beauty, but challenge and adventure of such power that all canoemen dream some day of penetrating its vastnesses.

Stretching still farther northwest lie the Yukon and Alaska with their high mountains, glaciers, and tundras. While few of the old voyageurs *ever saw this remote land, they knew it was there beyond the utmost reaches of the* pays d'en haut.

CHAPTER 12

JUMPING-OFF PLACES

IN THE NORTH, starting points for expeditions have always been known as jumping-off places. How far that usage goes I do not know, but imagine it was born long ago when men were still pushing ahead of the frontiers. I like the connotation of the phrase; it is down to earth and means what it says. Even in these days of aerial maps and photographs, if the goal is new country, one is never sure exactly what lies ahead no matter how thoroughly briefed. Though rapids may be marked, they are unpredictable until you see them, and while storms may be no different, perhaps, than storms anywhere else, they will be encountered in strange terrain. Beginnings are jumping-off places into unknown country.

I always look over the gear and the crew before takeoff, survey the clean outfits, the bulging packs, the untanned faces, realizing that in a short time all will be changed: clothes torn, sweat-stained, and spattered with mud and grease, faces fly-bitten and scratched, canoes, packs, tents patched and worn and everyone just a bit wiser than when he went in.

There is a certain something in the air at the beginning of a trip. One is perhaps a little more alive and aware than at any other time during the expedition and, because one is aware, somehow everything stands out in sharper focus and seemingly insignificant things are important. Life at those moments is good and full of challenge and, without being conscious of it, men feel, possibly, a touch of romance and derring-do that colors all about them. At least, so it is with me. The slate is fresh and clean then without the marks which might later blur the picture.

I have picked at random three jumping-off places, scattered from the Hudson Bay country to Great Slave Lake in the far northwest. Why I chose these three from those I have known, I do not know, except perhaps that each is somewhat different in its impact and measures up in my memory to what such places should really mean.

The first was the Indian settlement at Pukatawagan Narrows on the lower Churchill River a few hundred miles from its outlet in the Bay. After interminable postponements, the train finally dropped us off at a siding. It was an hour before midnight but we had made the decision to get under way immediately to make up for lost time. Dark figures emerged from the bush. They helped us take canoes and packs out of the baggage car, the last barely out the door before the red lantern flashed its signal. The train began to move, a farewell whistle, and it was on its way to The Pas.

"Start now?" queried one of the Indians. "Pretty dark."

"Yes," I said, "we'll portage to the lake, push down a few miles toward South Indian."

There was no reply. Had he known we had no guide, or that none of us had ever seen this stretch of the mighty Churchill, he would have been puzzled. In any case, starting down such a waterway at night instead of waiting for morning seemed strange.

We threw on packs and canoes, made the short carry to the water's edge, loaded, and were off into the dusk. The Indians with their dogs followed us, stood silently at the muddy landing. This did not happen every night, would be something to talk about for days to come.

It was good to be in the canoes again, canoes that a year before had been left at Norman Wells on the Mackenzie over a thousand miles to the northwest. They moved with no effort, slipping swiftly through the water as though glad to be on the river once more.

As we rounded the first point, I looked back at the dark crowd of Indians on the shore, at the spruces etched against a still rosy sky and the stars beginning to show. Then the dogs began their howling until the lake echoed and re-echoed with a weird and tremulous music of which we seemed a part. The chorus finally faded, merged with the swish of paddles and the soft gurgle of bows against the water.

The prelude was ended but it only set the stage for what was to come. When we started I had noticed a faint brightening over the horizon, but had concluded it was just the afterglow. Now the northern lights came out in full-fledged streamings and zigzag curtains, dancing across the blueblack of the heavens in all the hues of the spectrum. We paddled on into a blazing and shifting panorama that was not only in the skies but reflected in the water around us. For an hour the lights played; and, spellbound, we went on with no thought of the passage of time.

Ahead was an opening that looked like a channel, but soon it became shallow and choked with vegetation. Ducks rose in alarm, quacked loudly, whispered by overhead. A blind bay; we would have to return and follow them down the river. This we did, still watching the aurora, skirting rocky shores, looking for a place flat enough to pitch our tents. The water quickened. Our canoes were in the current at last, and we swung into a tiny island in midstream and found the rocks were level enough to land.

I built a fire and cooked a pot of tea, and then we crawled wearily into our bags. The lights were gone now, the stars bright, the only sound the soft swish of the current on either side of the island. That jumping-off place had been a symphony of sound and color from the moment the canoes were launched beside the railroad until we found our campsite.

Not every start has such a prelude. It may be something else which leaves an aura of the unusual, a decision perhaps, or the feeling that a particular expedition is going to be different. That is how it was with us when we came to the south end of Reindeer Lake in northern Saskatchewan on our way to Athabasca.

The canoes had spent the winter there stored in a log warehouse of the Hudson's Bay Company. The Indians had come down to the dock as usual to see us off, examine our mound of equipment and supplies, look critically at the Peterboroughs lying on the grass. This time we were faced with a major decision that in itself heightened our awareness just as the howling dogs and the northern lights did at Pukatawagan. Reindeer with its thousands of islands was a hundred and fifty miles in length, and we must traverse two thirds of it to the north in order to reach the mouth of the Swan River leading toward Athabasca. There were tremendous open sweeps and, if a gale should develop, we could be pinned down for days, in spite of protecting islands and channels. I looked at the glittering expanse sparkling in the sunlight. The breeze was behind us, soft and balmy, just strong enough to urge us on our way, but it could shift in an hour's time as it had on Amisk, Dead, Namew, and we could be fighting combers. The lake looked beautiful and inviting. It would be a challenge to head out boldly and go with the wind.

To the west of Reindeer was a parallel inland route with little creeks, ponds, and lakes which also led directly to the Swan. It could be tough going, portages, fly-infested ponds, shallow and choked with weeds. With the season we had had, the rapids could be almost dry. It would take as much time as paddling Reindeer itself, and there was a chance of being bogged down in some swampy morass.

We spread the big map out on the dock and studied it intently. The inland route stood clear and it went where we wanted to go. Still, Reindeer was a straight shot.

"How about it?" I asked one of the Indians.

He took a swift look at the map, laughed, and shrugged his shoulders. "Mebbe," he said, "mebbe all right, mebbe no water."

I turned to Omond, but his face was impassive, I looked around hopefully for some sign from the others.

"It's up to you," said Omond, "we'll do whatever you say."

Once long ago I had read a story by James Oliver Curwood about Reindeer, a fantastic tale of Mounties pursuing outlaws and of a girl with golden hair. The details of that thriller are forgotten, but not the picture of Reindeer itself, its crystal-clear waters, its white glaciated shores against the blue. Those polished spits of granite would mean gorgeous campsites all the way, with vistas and sunsets. We would miss all that if we followed the muskeg route to the west.

"We'll take the big lake," I said, "I've a hunch our luck will hold."

Without more ado, we loaded the canoes and headed toward a cluster of islands lying to the north. That first hour I wondered whether we had made the right choice, but with the canoes barreling along, I became absorbed in the sheer joy of movement. It was one of the most beautiful days any of us had ever known in the north and we made thirty miles to our first camp with little effort, a site from which we could feast our eyes on distance. It was calm that evening, reflections floated everywhere, and mirages lay against the open horizon.

For three days the wind held, but skirting a final point before entering the mouth of the Swan, it shifted to the west and as we pushed up the first fast water toward the divide between Reindeer and Wollaston, we watched combers building up in the open, combers which might have stopped us had we delayed.

Now I can look back at that jumping-off place and the decision we faced, knowing its very uncertainty etched indelibly the beauty around us. It was the same as shooting a rapids the first time, the tightening of muscles and nerves to the point where every rock and swirl seems more distinct. At such moments even the song of a bird heard above the rushing can be so clear, it is never heard again without remember-

ing. Reindeer was like that. One can forget lakes and portages midway through an expedition, when experiences com-
pound themselves and are lost through a great blending
and confusion of impressions, but never entirely those at the
start.

The third jumping-off place was at the start of an expedition along the Camsell River to Great Bear and the Mackenzie, the farthest north our canoes had ever been. To the south
was the bold, rocky coast of Great Slave Lake with its many
islands and enormous vistas leading east and west. To the
north was a bleak and barren land once occupied by a tribe
known as the Yellow Knives, natives who in the long ago had
fashioned spears and knives from the strange yellow metal
they found in the Coppermine region to the northeast. Now
they were gone toward the west, and the land lay deserted
and alone.

We were on the shore of a little lake, had chosen a campsite
on a glaciated point. The rocks were strewn with equipment
and supplies and we hurried, for the sun was dropping swiftly.
It was a wan, yellow sun, masses of dark clouds hemming it
in. A thin stand of spruces straggled bravely up the high
slopes around us, then gave way to lichens, mosses, and scrub
brush.

There was plenty of room for the tents, a good cooking spot
close to the water. Quickly I found the kettle pack, emptied
its contents on a poncho, placed the grate across two rocks,
and with twigs from a dead spruce started the fire. It flared

instantly and we were at home once more. The food packs were also dumped and I selected what I needed for supper—luxuries that first night, beans, ham, tinned fruit, fresh bread, and tea—chose an eating place nearby, laid out cups, plates, and tools. I was so busy I did not notice Denis standing behind me.

"Bourgeois," he said casually, "I think there are about 240 all told and allowing for a few still flying around who can't make up their minds, I should probably add another ten per cent. Let's see," he mumbled, "that would make it about 275 or thereabouts."

"What on earth are you mumbling about?" I asked without looking up.

"Flies," he explained patiently, "bulldogs, the big ones that take off a pound of flesh in a bite, black gnats—the bleeders who are more polite, mosquitoes, deer flies, and sundry other varmints."

I stirred the beans now coming to a boil, turned the ham, moved the teapot to one side.

"Just how," I asked, "did you arrive at such a figure?"

"Well," he said, "it really was easy. You've got your checkered shirt on which is a sort of a grid, and all I did was count the number on each square and multiply. Twenty squares with a dozen or so per square would make it 240 and as I said, ten per cent additional for transients would make it close to 275.

"It looks like a good trip, Bourgeois," he said cheerfully,

picking up the axe. "If the weather stays nice and warm, we'll be eaten alive before we reach Great Bear."

I knew what the fly situation could be in this country, portages intolerable, and camps as well. I stood up, shrugged my shoulders and the air was full of buzzing and wings. I looked at the backs of my hands and they were covered too. The others had also been too busy to comment. Tents were going up, sleeping bags, air beds, personal gear strewn all over the rocks. Elliot was brushing a cloud away from his head, Denis calmly chopping tent poles.

The sun dropped below the horizon. Suddenly it was cold and the flies were gone. We ate supper quietly, but there wasn't the usual banter at a first camp. Somehow the realization we were heading into the high north for the first time, and into conditions we had never experienced before, surrounded us. Gales would be blowing off the Arctic Coast, spray freezing on paddles, and if we had to line and wade, the cold would be bitter indeed. If anything happened, we would be far from help.

I glanced over the shoreline, thin, ragged spruces reaching for the sky, ledges covered only with caribou moss. One of the slopes where a fire had swept some years before was as desolate as the surface of the moon. Different from the Churchill, Reindeer, Athabasca, this land was savage, bleak and cold.

The canoes lay near the water. They were scarred and patched, had gouges in the gunwales, bulges along the sides, the same old Prospectors that had carried us so many wilderness miles. They would run new rapids now, ride the waters of sub-arctic lakes. It was reassuring to see them there, they were so familiar, so much a part of all the trips we had made. If all went well, they would reach Eldorado on the Bear, and then the Mackenzie some five hundred miles to the northwest. This was no summer holiday with swimming before supper, or drifting along with our shirts off enjoying the sun. If a canoe should overturn, the situation could be desperate.

I prayed for an impossible favor—good weather: cold enough to stop the flies, for winds that would permit crossing of the larger waters without hazard. To me that night, a pall seemed to lie over the land that colored rocks, trees, and water, as well as my own spirit. The gray shores, the leaden waters, the stark, almost barren hills crushed in on me with overpowering menace. That night it was the apprehension of what lay ahead that heightened my perceptions and brought everything into sharp and indelible focus. Danger and hazard strangely enough have the same impact as beauty and delight.

I do not embark on any expedition now without being aware of those jumping-off places of the past. No beginning, no matter how trivial, is ever unimportant to me. I look forward to the new ones and treasure those I have known. They are vignettes of experience whose brightness never fades, moments when life and everything around me have special clarity and meaning.

CHAPTER 13

THE PAYS PLAT

WEST OF Port Arthur, between the port and Nipigon, lies the Pays Plat. Someone had mentioned trout in the stream and I pictured just another river with a bridge of steel and concrete. It would look, I imagined, like any one of the many beautiful streams along the north shore of Lake Superior, brawling down from the highlands through black, desperate gorges with swirling foam-laced pools below them, the inevitable sand bars at the mouth where they emptied into the broad, slow wash of the lake.

When we reached the Pays Plat all thoughts of fishing left me for here was a vision of the past, of the days before the road. Long ago the *voyageurs* of the fur brigades, in their great Montreal canoes, following the treacherous shoal areas of the coast from St. Ignace Island to Thunder Bay, had given it that name. It means relatively flat, low country. The valley through which the river ran was a green, open meadow, spruce trees hemming it in where the hills came down. An old church and a graveyard lay close to the road, the stones covered with moss and lichens. Crude picket fences guarded some of the graves.

Cars roared beside them now, traffic toward the famous Nipigon, Terrace Bay, Michipicoten, and to the cities of the east. While we were there it was raining. Mist covered the valley and for a moment the sound of motors was gone. The valley of the Pays Plat was quiet, as it used to be.

Upstream and on either side of the river were scattered log cabins, the homes of those who, after living in the wilderness of the back country, were hungry for the warmth of old friendships and the waves of Lake Superior. My thoughts went back to a world of long ago, when neither the road nor the cities of Port Arthur and Duluth were even thought of. The Pays Plat was then a mission and a trading post for the Indians and French who trapped and gathered furs and lived their simple, primitive lives.

Now fishermen come with strange equipment, hip boots, baskets and rods, to fish for speckled trout below the rapids and the falls. They arrive in beautiful cars, camp along the shore, take pictures of the quaint weather-beaten church and the cabins; some have great trailer houses larger than the cabins themselves. There are hundreds everyday, and the roar never ends. Always in a hurry, they are going east and west as though their lives depended on speed, as though it were wrong to stay too long. At night their fires are bright along the lake and sometimes they gather around them to sing.

While I stood there I heard a woman singing, over by the church, a song I had heard that very morning over my radio at Port Arthur. The voice was soft and melodious and I recognized the minor key and the quaver of the Chippewa though the old song she sang was strange to those of Indian blood. "South of the Border" was the tune, a song of the Rio Grande and Mexico, two thousand miles away. I listened with amazement and surprise and then I saw the girl, dressed as many Indians are close to the settlements: a pair of slacks, a colorful blouse and moccasins, her black hair tied with a ribbon. On her back was a papoose in its traditional basket or *ahtikanagon*. She was sitting on a rock at the river's edge, looking around as though waiting for someone to come. Stooping, the girl picked up a handful of pebbles, threw them one by one into the pool before her, still singing of a desert land she had never seen. She worked her way downstream in spite of the rain, then took a trail back to one of the cabins and disappeared.

My fishing was forgotten. Somehow it did not seem important any more. I put my rod back into its case and strolled over to the churchyard and, among the graves, noted the French and Indian names. All of that was gone, like the mist that would soon lift from the valley, gone as the swirling waters under the bridge.

A roar from behind me, and a shiny black car sped by on its way to Nipigon. A woman with dark glasses and a blonde pony-tail was intent on a travel folder, did not give the river a glance. I knew what the folder said for I had picked one up at the tourist information center at Port Arthur: "Fish the famous Nipigon"—the Pays Plat merely mentioned, nothing there but an old Indian village and a church.

That day I felt part of the past, and within me was a certain sadness and nostalgia for all that was disappearing. I could not forget the Indian girl and her song. As we, too, drove along the beautiful highway overlooking Lake Superior with its vistas of rocky headlands to the east, all I thought of was brigades of fur canoes coming down those blue, sparkling reaches from Montreal, and those returning from Grand Portage with fur from the far northwest. The road seemed strange, the cars and bridges, the hurrying, well-dressed tourists who knew nothing of the past. All this had come about within a hundred years. In that time canoes had given way to sailing ships and steam, to automobiles and airplanes. In that time we had fought two major wars, had discovered space time, reached the moon, and our population had pyramided to the point of danger to the race. No longer was there isolation. All peoples and countries were now accessible either by modern transport or through the medium of radio.

The Chippewa girl singing "South of the Border" along the Pays Plat was symbolic of the transition that was taking place not only there but all over the north. But I knew, in spite of her song, she was still rooted in the past, part of the old mission and the graveyard, part of the era of *voyageurs* and of the long centuries before the white man came. Changes had come but she still listened to the slow wash of the surf, and lived in her dream world as her people had always done. The ballad was just a tune to her.

I thought of other places close to the past where changes have come in the last ten years, Ile à la Crosse on the Churchill, Yellowknife on Great Slave, Stony Rapids on Lake Athabasca, Fort Franklin on Great Bear, Nelson House on the Burntwood, even Fort Yukon below the ramparts of the Brooks Range in Alaska. In the Eskimo country young people danced to Rock-and-Roll and sang hillbilly songs. Old songs were being forgotten for the new.

The day before, I had visited the Indian village of Grand Portage, one of the most famous names along the north shore of Lake Superior, now a National Monument. Once a thriving metropolis of trade, the old stockade of the Northwest Company had been rebuilt and a building within it now served as a museum. I climbed the hill above the post where lookouts once watched for the appearance of fur brigades coming around Hat Point a mile to the southeast, Hat Point with its gnarled Witches Tree, an ancient cedar that had seen it all. As I sat there I forgot the new stockade, the museum, the sight-seeing tourists, and looked over the scene below as Daniel Harmon had over one hundred and fifty years before. Walter O'Meara in his book *Grand Portage* tells it well.

"Daniel Harmon," he said, "looked down upon Grand Portage Bay from the summit of Sugar Loaf. He had climbed up to this place because one could see so far. On a clear day you could see the breakers on the shore of Isle Royale. You could look across the bay beyond the Pointe au Chapeau to where a fleet of little islands screened the rocky coast. It was among these islands that you first caught the flash of paddles when the canoes from Montreal arrived.

"Daniel looked down moodily at the swarming scene below. He noted how like a firesteel was the outline of Grand Portage Bay with Pointe au Chapeau on one horn, Pointe à la Framboise on the other, the small wooded island across the open edge. . . . Directly below him clustered the canoe yards, the stockade, and the buildings of the Northwest Company Post.

"It was a very ancient place and no one among the Nor'-westers knew who first had come to it. . . . Somewhere in the desolate up country—the pays d'en haut—he would spend the next seven years of his life. . . . Solitude and silence would surround him. Often he would be without books, without friends, or even enemies who spoke his tongue."

A few years earlier I had camped on the beach below and had carried the famous nine-mile portage around the rapids of the Pigeon on the way to Fort Lac la Pluie almost three

hundred miles away. I did it as it had been done in earlier
times and, in the doing, somehow became one with the days
of trade and adventure, part of their grueling toil and hardship, part of the flies and of the heat and cold, of the danger,
part of the solitudes and loneliness of the unbroken distances
that used to be.

The right of way lay in back of the village and its burial
ground, soared in wide, sweeping curves toward the Pigeon,
crossed the historic portage over a deep fill of broken rock
and gravel. I stopped there and looked down some twenty
feet to where the trail emerged from the bush, the trail that
once had struck fear into the hearts of all *voyageurs* going
into the back country. I could see the long files of heavily
laden men toiling up the slope from Lake Superior lying blue
and sparkling in the distance, glanced to the north and caught
for a moment the joy in the eyes of men coming down from
the other end, men who had spent a year or more in the
Athabasca country of the far northwest and now were on
their way to a rendezvous at Grand Portage Post.

I drove on to Mount Josephine where an eighty-foot gap
had been blasted through the rock to allow the highway to
pass, skirted the round jewel of Teal Lake, once a hidden
haunt of moose and ducks, now only a chance for Koda-
chromes. From a lookout at the base of the high ridge separating Grand Portage valley from that of the Pigeon, I could
see the Susie Islands and the dim outline of Isle Royale eighteen miles away. Beyond that was the Nipigon and the way

to the east. For the first time in history, people could encircle Lake Superior and penetrate a wilderness that until now had changed little since the days of the trade.

I walked back to where I had left my car at the Pays Plat bridge and drove on, became lost in vistas of rocky islands and precipitous shores with waves dashing high against them, but all the time I was conscious of the past, the rapidity of change, what it was doing to the girl on the Pays Plat and to thousands of others at posts and villages all over the north. Airplanes now kept in daily contact, and supplies came in with enormous tractor trains when lakes and rivers and tundra were frozen solid. No longer was there any excuse for starvation, disease, or ignorance. A new era was dawning. It should be a time of hope and confidence for the future, but I wondered, knowing how slowly people change. Though outwardly they seemed to adapt to new ways of life, inwardly there was unrest.

On a recent expedition, I had stopped at Nelson House, a community of perhaps a thousand Indians, some two hundred and fifty miles west of the mouth of the Nelson River on Hudson Bay. There was much activity there, remodeling of the old Post and the construction of a Sunday school. I went into the building with the young rector of the church. Here was modern design with all the conveniences of an annex to some church in town. Power saws and drills were busy, and carpenters crawled around the scaffolding fitting into place boards, plywood, wiring, and insulation that had been flown in or brought by tractor train the winter before. There would be a playroom, a nursery, a central gathering place with large windows to give a view of the river. It would be delightful when finished, a real addition to the church life of the community. With the population increasing, the rector said, it was necessary to do something for the children.

I went up to the old Hudson's Bay Company post. The storekeeper explained, it too was being enlarged and remodeled, would soon have a display section, be a self-help establishment like that of any shopping center below. Gone would be the old spirit of trading, gone the intimate, personal responsibility of a factor for the people.

The store was crowded, some of the Indians old, but most of them in their teens, girls in slacks, boys in leather jackets and some with duck-tail haircuts, small children with shoes instead of moccasins. I bought some candy and passed it around but it made little impression. A girl came in with allotment money and bought a box of canned goods, another, six cans of fruit and a handful of candy bars, all paid for in cash. My gesture was of little importance. There seemed to be no shortage of money and, of a sudden, I felt that what I had done was slightly ridiculous and out of place.

Nelson House was far from the railroad. There was nowhere for young people to go, nothing to do. There were still a few trappers; one of them, the factor told me, had brought in five thousand dollars worth of fur the winter before; but mostly such industry did not appeal. The young people lounged around and waited, listening to the radio with news of the outside. Some of the older boys dreamed of going down the river to the new mining town at Thompson but, when they did, they returned swiftly to talk of their exploits, spend the money they had earned. They could always go back for another try when the call of adventure was too strong to resist. There was no interest any more in learning the craft of their people or how to survive in the bush. That was all old-fashioned. This was a new and easier way to live.

Never before had they been so well taken care of, with so much food, protection, or security. No longer did they have to go on long expeditions following the caribou or the trapping lines. That was for those who did not know better. Far safer and more pleasant to stay close to the church and the post, knowing that a benevolent government would not let them starve, get sick, or suffer undue hardships.

Up in the Eskimo country northwest of Fort Churchill, on a caribou-banding expedition, the Eskimos and Indians kept in constant touch with the outside world by radio, listened with delight to the music. I can hear them laugh, hum the tunes, follow the games, make bets on their outcomes. Montreal, Winnipeg, Toronto and Detroit, those were places where life really went on. True, they were packing, paddling, living out-of-doors as their forebears had done, but their food was white man's food, and after the tagging was over they would fly to Baker Lake, to The Pas, to Fort Churchill on the Bay.

Once during a reconnaisance survey of the interior of Alaska, our plane landed at Fort Yukon, one of the most remote landing strips in the north. We were met by an Indian boy on a motor scooter. He raced out along the runway in a cloud of dust, met us with as much of a flourish as though he were driving a team of huskies. He wore a leather jacket with silver studs, a bright visored cap, cowboy boots; long yellow streamers flew from his handlebars. This was life and all he wanted; his, a job that satisfied completely.

That evening I walked along the historic Yukon, the great brown river that for two thousand miles winds its way from the gold rush country of Dawson Creek and the Klondike to the Bering Sea and the enormous delta marshes of its tidal mouth. I stopped beside a fish wheel turning slowly in the brown current, watched an Indian woman retrieve her catch from the weir into which the wheel dropped its load. There were two large fish, a couple of salmon, one for the dogs, the other for the pot. The sunset was violent over the river and for a moment the woman stood in black silhouette against its glow. It was late in the season; before long the snows would come.

At Fort Norman on the Mackenzie, Indians were building snug new houses with windows, insulation, and room. A huge walk-in deep freeze had been installed and at first was full of meat, but now that most of the moose had been killed nearby, it was becoming increasingly difficult to keep it stocked. Again a benevolent government had made all things possible, but there were more and more Indians with nothing to do, no place to go but outside.

All over the north it is the same, even in the far-off DEW Line stations along the Arctic Coast, a swift changing of the old way of life with little to take its place. True, there is physical security for the first time, but something has been lost, a certain identification with the past, the almost cosmic sense of an ancient primitive race with its totems, its symbolism, the sense of living in a stabilized ecological complex. Gone seems to be the old feeling of being a part of the earth and all its processes. Spiritual roots have been cut and replaced by a world of gadgetry, speed, and excitement in which the old ways are unimportant. Lost is the wisdom of a people.

The girl on the Pays Plat, the teen-agers at Nelson House, the Eskimo and Swampy Crees on Nejanilini, the boy at Fort Yukon, are all typical. Somehow the transition must be made, and I wonder if after all the answer is in building again on their inherent dignity, respect for a land they love and for a way of life which is part of them no matter what they do. True, they could never return as a people to doing things as they were done in the past, but in the process of change they might keep the best of their own traditions, use what they can of ours and, with guidance, avoid our evils. We might with patience and understanding give them a vision of freedom and the right to work out their own destiny in a creative way that would build rather than destroy not only them, but also the land to which they still belong.

I wonder, now that so many of them are concentrated at villages, posts, and missions, with enormous areas lying almost deserted where once they used to roam, if perhaps in these broad reaches of the old wilderness may not be a partial answer to their problem of adjustment to the new way of life.

They have much to give that civilization needs. Theirs is a country of great beauty, solitude, and remoteness, a land teeming with game and fish. They are native to this land and within them, in spite of what has happened, is a deep and inherent sense of oneness and belonging. They could teach us much we need to learn, could contribute to the culture and happiness of millions who, because of the expansion in population and growing urbanization, have been deprived of the very things that are now considered by Indians and Eskimos to be of little worth.

It may well be that with their help the Canadian north, with its vast expanses of primeval country, can restore to modern man a semblance of balance and completeness. In the long run, these last wild regions of the continent might be worth far more to North Americans from a recreational and spiritual standpoint than through industrial exploitation. If this vision could be realized, even in part, these people might once more be proud of their heritage.

CHAPTER 14

GHOST CAMPS OF THE NORTH

T HE *voyageurs* of our expedition had battled their way up the Camsell River from the height of land above Great Slave toward the barren bleakness of Great Bear. It was a time of rain and cold; the winds off the arctic ice never ceased. The terrain had grown more and more rugged, and each day we fought the waves, dodged behind islands, and skirted dangerous promontories we could not avoid. We ran what rapids our canoes could take, but when they were bad, portaged, for in that icy water we dared not take a chance.

The hills were almost mountainous now, great glaciated masses of rock, the ragged growth of spruce all but gone except along the lake shores and in the valleys of connecting

157

streams. It was a savage land and full of beauty, even where the fires had been and billowing ridges of granite lay bare to pitiless gales.

Not a soul had we seen since our trip began, no Indians or vestiges of their camps. They had migrated long ago to the milder climate of the Mackenzie Valley to the west. There was more game to hunt, riverboats and barges passed constantly on their way to Norman Wells and Aklavik, and activity was never lacking around the Hudson's Bay posts and the missions. The Camsell lay deserted as though the glacier had just retreated. So accustomed had we been to seeing no one, it was with great excitement we saw something strange on the opposite shore of a lake on the way to Hottah.

We got out the glasses and studied it intently. It was a wrecked plane, a DC-3 lying at a crazy angle against the bank, with one wing much lower than the other, behind it several cabins, possibly a mine or some trader's outfit. Quickly we changed course and headed toward it. That low wing meant trouble and in the north a downed plane is never ignored. As we neared, we studied it again. There was no mistake, the craft was lying close against the rocky shore.

We pushed swiftly now and on the way passed a little island, its bare surface completely covered with a mat of orange lichen. I could not resist taking a color shot as we passed, a spot of orange with tufts of golden grass against the leaden background of the lake. We landed at what had once been a dock. The planks were broken now, the piling loose and tilted. The aircraft was only a shell, one motor gone, the other a wreck, the interior stripped and dismantled. The loading door hung on its hinges and creaked in the wind. The tipped wing was supported by a crib of logs. There was nothing to salvage, it would stay there for a long time, gleaming against the shore. We walked up the well-beaten trail to one of the cabins, opened the unlocked door and stepped inside.

This was the cook shack, the table set for twenty men. Bread and butter were still there, meat, mashed potatoes, jelly and jam. A pumpkin pie with one wedge missing stood at the end. The gravy bowl was full, the sliced bread and cake hard. Nothing had been touched or molested, no signs of squirrels, mice, or rats, no decay or spoilage. It was as though the men had left the day before in the midst of a meal.

I went into the kitchen, its shelves stocked with food, hundreds of dollars worth, enough to keep the crew going for months, tinned supplies precious in this far country, vegetables, strawberries, peaches, tinned meats, and sausage. In a back lean-to hung a dried up haunch of moose, a hide, and a slab of bacon. Shining utensils hung on the walls: pots and pans, knives, skillets, spoons. Nothing was out of place.

We left and walked into the next building, the office of the engineer and superintendent. On a drafting table was an unfinished sketch of the mining property, a file for letters and plans. I thumbed through the file; the last letter was dated at the close of the Korean war. A uranium mine, it had been discontinued when rich prospects close to civilization no longer warranted its operation. A mahogany box contained a new theodolite in a velvet case. It had never been used and was worth a great deal of money. Surveying instruments stood in a corner, drill bits, flat iron strips and bars were laid neatly on separate racks.

The men's quarters and bunkhouses were the same, items of personal equipment, gloves, shirts, rain gear and boots, all left behind in the hurry of departure. On a small table beside one of the bunks I picked up a cluster of quartz crystals. Some were stained with iron, some the color of old rose, others close to amethyst. They were clear and well shaped. On one crystal was a deposit of silver, between two other faces a tiny speck of the same orange lichen we had seen on the little island in crossing the lake. Since it was a perfect specimen, I picked it up, dropped it into my pocket. It is before me now as I write and brings the scene of that abandoned mining camp back to me.

We returned to the cook shack, sat down at the table with the uneasy feeling that the men who had been there last were still around, the cook busying himself in the kitchen before his stove, the *cookee* bringing in the food, seeing the gravy was hot, the teapot full. None of us spoke. This was a place of ghosts. We closed the door carefully so no animals would get in. Ten years, or a hundred, it would make little difference in that frigid climate.

Back in the engineer's office, we picked up the theodolite and placed it carefully in one of the half-empty packs. It was very heavy, but none of us could bear the thought of leaving it behind. We would drop it off eventually at Eldorado on Great Bear.

We took some tinned fruit and meat, went back to the canoes, pushed off toward the lichen-covered rock and east toward our rendezvous on Great Bear. As we rounded the last point, I turned and looked back. There was the gleam of silver, behind it the dark cluster of cabins, the table still set, the engineer's shack, the bunkhouses, the hopes and dreams of men who had lived and perhaps died there. Too costly to fly out, the camp was left as many others were in the far reaches of the north. Some day, should the demand warrant, it might open again, but now it was better lost and forgotten.

Not until we reached Eldorado did we know the story, how one of the supply planes had gone through the crust of spring ice and hurtled into the bank. One wing had been almost sheared, an engine ruined, the fuselage twisted out of shape—no casualties, just one of those accidents that happen to bush pilots all over the north. The men had saved what they could, but there the wreck would stay until the elements corroded the aluminum and it finally sank into the water and muck along the shore.

Two years later I came across another ghost camp almost a thousand miles to the southeast. It was during the course of a caribou survey where the endless tundra bordering Hudson Bay meets the scraggly line of the Taiga, that land of stunted spruce, muskeg, and caribou moss that extends not only through our own north but across all of Siberia as well. The migration was on, and we were flying in to join a research party tagging the caribou in an attempt to determine how they moved.

From the air, Duck Lake Post of the Hudson's Bay Company looked like any other on the tundra, or for that matter anywhere in the north, a white building with a red roof, a cluster of storage sheds and shacks, a warehouse for furs and supplies, canoe racks, a little dock. Built on a bare point of land between Duck Lake and Nejanilini, it once served the scattered bands of Swampy Crees and even some of the Eskimo of the Wolverine-Seal River country, as far west as Nueltin and east to Hudson Bay. It was isolated enough so travelers seldom came and, when they did, it was a momentous event.

But this time there was no running about, no waving or frantic preparations for our arrival, no smoke from the chimneys, no tents or shelters around the post or canoes pulled up on the shore, no dogs straining at their chains and howling their hearts out in the excitement of our landing. Not a soul was to be seen anywhere, only a lone fox streaking across the point for the cover of the willow fringe beyond. We swung low to be sure of the approach, buzzed the little gray deserted church across the bay. It was weather-beaten, with the windows gone and grass growing around its steps. The cross was at an angle leaning away from the wind.

We landed a quarter of a mile out in the lake, taxied cautiously to the dock. The outer cribbing was broken by the ice, the planking torn apart. We had difficulty in warping the Norseman into position because of sharp, protruding rocks, but finally tied it fast and walked up the trail to the main building. The Hudson's Bay Company sign was gone, nothing to indicate ownership. The store was still in good repair but the shelves were empty. I went into the kitchen and started a fire in the stove. It smoked at first, but after the debris and soot burned out it drew well. The coffee pot, kettles, and skillets were clean and we used them rather than get out our own. Supper was served in the small dining room where the factor had eaten many times with guests who came to visit. Beds and bunks were still in place in the attic. Some of us bedded down there.

I decided to sleep in the warehouse beside the old fur press. I wanted to be alone there to catch, perhaps, the feeling of the days when Duck Lake Post was alive. It was dark when I went over, and the great door complained when I put my shoulder against it and pushed it in. I lit a stub of a candle and placed it on a shelf, laid out my bag in the center and close to the open door, lay there in the flickering candlelight surveying my abode. To one side was a beaten-up freighter canoe long unused, on the other the press, a huge one with a great screw turned by an iron bar. Into that press had gone the fur to be made up into bales for the trip down the Wolverine to South Indian, or down the Seal to the Bay. Along the walls were shelves for storage, and rows of hooks for hides. I could see it in the spring after the fur was in, foxes and wolves, muskrats and beaver, wolverine, mink, and otter. I could smell it, too, for even though the hides were long gone, their pungence remained, an almost fetid and musky smell, a combination of all the creatures trapped in the north. Here, years before, lay the wealth of the region, the result of un-counted days and months of labor, privation, and danger. It had once held food and traps and equipment for all the sur-rounding native bands. This was more than a warehouse for fur and supplies, it was a bastion of security for all who lived within range.

I blew out the candle finally and went to sleep. Not a sound disturbed me all night long; no howling of huskies, no scurry-ing of mice or squirrels. I wakened once and listened, but there was only the lap of the waves down at the shore. The night was cloudy and dark and though I had braced the door with a stout log, it creaked in the rising wind.

In the morning to my joy the sun was out and I went onto the ramp to dress and to lace my boots. The planks were hand-hewn, shaped with axe and knife and rasp and held to-gether with wooden dowel pins. That approach to the great door was made to last. Up it had come bales and boxes from the canoes and boats and sleds, and down had gone the pressed bales of fur. I threw on my parka, went down to the shore and washed in the icy water, then walked down the length of the peninsula. The stakes that marked the tents were still in place and, with them, the debris of all Indian camps, shreds of cloth, worn moccasins, torn rubbers, the whitened, well-gnawed bones of caribou.

It seemed to me I could almost hear the Indians talking, could smell their fires, sense the coming and going. The country itself was the same. The barren tundra stretched endlessly in all directions, and marching up the hills were the scattered spruce of the Taiga in which the caribou sought shelter from winter storms. The lake sparkled in the sunshine as it had for thousands of years, the land itself as beautiful and full of meaning and challenge as it had ever been. Something was gone, however, a certain something that had been there before. It was Duck Lake Post that had changed with its abandonment.

I stood at the far end of the spit looking back toward the post with its rising plume of smoke, picturing it as it used to be when the smoke of many fires hung like a haze over the entire point. Greetings, goodbyes, tales of high adventure, sadness, and joy—all these were gone.

I knew then that though one loves a land, one still needs the warmth of companionship with others of his kind and must not always travel alone. This was the truth, for I had ghost camps of my own and country haunted with memories of those who had been with me. One of these places was a little campsite at the mouth of the Range River where it empties into Low Lake in the Quetico-Superior country. No one but my partner and I had ever used this spot, for from the

165

water's edge it looked like a marshy flat; but actually beyond the fringe of alders it was high and dry, with the shelf of grass sheltered well by a broadly branching jackpine. Here we laid our sleeping bags and gear when the bluebill flight was on, and for many years knew such companionship as only those can who share some common joy.

The place for the fire was close to a shelf of gray rock in back of the pine, and at night, if we had any luck, the light shone on the blue and green of wingbars, and the branches of the jackpine were a tracery of black above us. We stored our food in a crevice of the rock and always tucked away some kindling for a quick fire there. The river wound behind us, an open road to the Range Lake country and the border, while to the south and west were the golden rice beds, with a stand of tall pines against the sunsets. The decoys were placed in the mouth of the river for sooner or later something always came by. I will never forget the breath-taking roar of a bunch of bluebills coming down the river, the canvas-ripping sound of them as they dipped. Sometimes mallards lifted out of the rice and headed up river. Jacksnipe always began the day with their cheeping, and after dawn flocks of snowbirds drifted across the mud flats bordering the channel.

For many years Dean and I used the place and we came to love its sights and sounds and smells and the joy of all these things together, but then one day he took the trail to another hunting ground and our joy was gone. For a while I went back alone as though he were still with me and I could hear his banter, then, and see him moving around as he used to do. When I lay in my sleeping bag on the grassy shelf, I was conscious of the depression beside me, and when a flock came over high, I could hear him whisper, "Listen—there'll be action in the morning."

After a time I no longer returned to my ghost camp. It was better, I thought, to keep it with memories that were mine alone. For me that little camp had become a place of dreams. Others may go there now and perhaps they are finding what I found and building associations of their own. And so it is with all country. While the meaning of wilderness never changes to those who understand it, it means even more if you have sunk your roots in deeply. No country can ever be bleak or forbidding if it has once been a part of the love and warmth of those who have shared it with you.

Whenever I travel the lake and river country of the north, I meet friends of other days. They are with me constantly on the campsites and I meet them on portages, and hear them everywhere. Never again will I travel the Rainy, the Churchill, the Camsell, the Bear, or the Burntwood, or any other routes without reliving adventures with companions who have been with me.

The terrain has a different meaning now, not only through what we shared, but because of what we had known that gave us the feeling of the land itself, its eras of the past, the time when the Canadian Shield came into being, when prehistoric seas laid down formations of Athabasca sandstone, the glacial periods of the last million years when the routes we traveled were shaped by the gouging of the ice, the crossing of Asiatics over Bering Strait and their slow filtration into the south, the days of explorers and *voyageurs,* up to the swiftly changing time of today. All this we had shared and lived over many thousands of miles until almost unconsciously the long history of the primitive country we had traversed was absorbed into our minds and thoughts. We had left no mark on the country itself, but the land had left its mark on us.

The smoke was still rising high from the kitchen of the old post. Breakfast must be ready and I hurried back. The wind was coming up and we still had far to go.

CHAPTER 15

CARIBOU

I HAD CLIMBED to the top of a low mound in the caribou country over a hundred miles north-west of Fort Churchill on Hudson Bay. On the barren lands that morning was the feel of being above timber line, so fresh and clean was the air, so sparkling the sunlight. But here there were no peaks, no background of snowy ranges, only end-lessly rolling ridges with scattered clumps of gnarled spruce between them. This is where the vast unbroken tundra of the north meets the jagged tree line known as the Taiga. As far as I could see was the autumn pattern of copper, bronze, and red against the speckled blue of myriads of pools, ponds, and lakes. The land looked as though a tremendous deluge of waters had so recently covered it, there was no time for it to flow away, which indeed was the truth, for underneath is the eternal permafrost that keeps all waters from draining. Because of the ice, only the top few inches of soil thaw enough during the short summer to support life. Then under an almost continuous sun, hordes of insects come forth, while flowers, heathers, and lichens and grasses all but explode in frantic growth before the descent of snow and bitter cold seals the land again in white.

This was the birthplace of the ice sheet that once lay two miles thick over the great Bay and whose lobes spread to the south until they covered over half the continent. The terrain had been shaped by glaciers, smoothed, gouged, and disarranged, and by the waters before me, almost as they were when the melting took place. To the north, and beyond this gathering place of the tremendous snows that had formed the ice, is the Arctic Sea and islands reaching almost to the Pole. Here are no trees, only the tundra—Eskimo country, all of it, the land of the musk ox, wolf, and caribou, of seals, whales, and polar bears along bleak and empty coasts.

Only a few hundred miles to the south, the character of the country changes, trees gradually increasing in number, spruce, tamarack, aspen, Arctic birch, and jackpine, until the valleys of the great rivers are lush with them and the mossy tundras give way to swamp and muskeg. There lie the Churchill, the Nelson, the Albany, and the Hayes, once routes of trade and exploration from the Bay. They spread out into beautiful island-studded lakes, with rapids in between them, and gorges where they cut through the granite roots of the Laurentians or the limestones of ancient seas. At last these mighty rivers slow and lose themselves in the broad tidal flats of Hudson Bay, the depression that may have been formed by the massive weight of the ice.

I could see the white tents of our camp on the shore of Lake Nejanilini where the caribou cross. The wind was rising and whitecaps were beginning to show in the narrows. Then from an Eskimo lookout on the point came a high clear call almost like the howl of a wolf. "Cariboooooooooo—Caribooooooooooooooo." Instantly figures ran to the canoes, and through my glasses I could see the dark heads of swimming caribou. The freighter canoes were pushed into the water, motors started, and they raced over the waves with such speed, they were almost hidden in spray. In a few moments they were close to the herd and the wildly tossing antlers. The animals scattered in fright. A canoe ran alongside a bull; a swift pass of the shepherd's crook and the animal was drawn by its neck to the gunwale, held there firmly while an ear was clipped with a tag carrying two orange ribbons. As the bull was released, it plunged desperately to escape, its flailing hooves and lurching almost upsetting the canoe. On to the others sped the taggers, until many caribou wore orange ribbons with identifying numbers.

Some of the caribou were now swimming back to the shore they had left, others toward our camp. Eventually they would get together again and the migration would continue toward Duck Lake to the east. They swam high, heads and shoulders well above the surface, so buoyant, it seemed as though they were treading water rather than swimming. A moose swims with only its head and the top of its hump visible, and so it is with the white-tailed deer, but these animals are different. Buoyed by a dense blanket of hollow hairs, they seem to float, and they use their broad, splayed hooves to such advantage, few animals in the north can equal them in speed and maneuverability.

The canoes were back at the shore, gas tanks being filled, lookouts hiking toward their posts. In the space of a couple of weeks, five hundred caribou had already been tagged, more than any year before. Even so, it represented only a small fraction of the great herds that once came down from the tundras into the Taiga or land of little sticks. This was early September and soon the animals would swing back for the rutting to the barrens from which they came. Then, with the first snows and storms, they would drift down once more to the ragged fringe of spruce for protection during the long winter months.

The caribou of the north have been losing ground for years and the Province of Manitoba sponsored this project in an attempt to find out not only how and why the caribou migrate but, if possible, other factors which might effect their decrease in numbers. I had been invited to observe this study by my friend Gerry Malaher, head of the Game Branch of the Provincial Government.

Joe Robertson, the biologist in charge of the study, told me that according to the last extensive aerial census, less than 300,000 animals remained, 60 per cent decline from the 670,-000 of barely a decade ago. Early figures indicated fantastic populations, some explorers estimated up to a hundred million, diaries told of herds coming across the tundras for weeks at a time in numbers that baffled description. As with the bison of the west, it was thought nothing could ever reduce them, but now something is happening to the caribou.

Reasons advanced for this alarming decline are fall out, over-killing by Indians and Eskimo, predation by wolves, disease cycles, starvation due to enormous fires that have destroyed the vegetation of feeding grounds, or a combination of them all. Estimates of the annual kill run close to thirty thousand, far more than their dwindling numbers can stand. This, coupled with other losses, makes the situation critical. The caribou are approaching the crisis the buffalo faced less than a century ago; the tagging is an attempt to find the answers before it is too late. The story of their migration and what happens to them enroute can be vital to their survival as a species.

I spent little time at camp or with the tagging crew, wandered instead over the barren lands. I wanted to get the feel of this area in contrast to the forested lake and river country to the south. For the past month and for almost five hundred miles, I had traveled by canoe down the Churchill, the Rat, and the Burntwood beyond Nelson House this side of the Bay. I was still full of the tumult of rapids, vistas of great lakes, rugged portages between them, and was so completely immersed in memories of my expedition it was exciting to be in a land where there were no forests, nothing to stop the view of endless and open terrain. It felt good to walk again, to stretch my legs and to get the sense of unlimited horizons.

I left the first low rise where I had seen the tagging, to follow the long peninsula separating Nejanilini from the Wolverine River and Duck Lake. This is the land where Indians and Eskimos meet, where the white fox, the lemming, and the Arctic hare meet the marten, beaver, and ermine from the forest transition zones to the south. While Eskimos used it in times past, it was really the ancestral hunting ground of their traditional enemies the Chipewyans, or caribou-eaters, still the most primitive and semi-nomadic Indians of the north.

For thousands of years this famous crossing place for the migrating bands of caribou had been known and fought over by native tribes. According to Gerry Malaher, Joe Robertson had found what he thought was a Sandia-type arrowhead at the Nejanilini site which, if authentic, could possibly date back far beyond the points of Folsom Man.

The killing was done from canoes or on the land after the caribou had swum across the narrows. Both Eskimos and Indians, experts in the art of handling a spear, always aim for the same spot behind the shoulder and close to the backbone. A quick thrust by the spearsman pierces the lung; the spear is withdrawn and the canoe speeds on to another victim. Few caribou swim more than a few strokes before collapsing.

If the killing were to be done on shore, the hunters placed mounds of stones on either side of the landing place and at intervals inland, guiding the animals gradually toward a funnel, where, bunched together they were easy prey to arrows or even spears. Sometimes women and children were placed between the piles of stones to frighten the caribou toward the place where the hunters waited. No doubt there was unnecessary slaughter during the early days when caribou were plentiful, but it made little difference then, as the endless herds came through as before with no apparent diminution in numbers.

But now, with the caribou population seriously depleted, killing more than is actually needed for food and clothing does make a great difference, and with the advent of the motor-driven canoe it is far easier to run down all the members of a band of swimming caribou and spear them before they can reach the shore. Not many years before, during a good migration, the shores of Nejanilini were piled high with bloated and unused carcasses. While the rifle may have increased the kill in certain areas, ammunition is still too costly to use where more primitive methods suffice.

The tundra was covered with bleached antlers, snow white

and beautiful. I stopped before three great racks close together, their palmate tips a strange and lovely pattern against the autumn colors. There were hundreds of them, possibly thousands, as the killing had gone on for many years. In that climate they disintegrated very slowly and, in spite of occasional small nibblings by mice, lemmings, and other creatures, the antlers remained intact. Cloud berries were yellow and juicy in low places, blueberries still holding on. They were small and bitter compared to those at home. Bilberries and cranberries were red, their leaves russet, copper, and orange. The flowers were gone, for this was just before the snows.

The walking was difficult, close to the water the soft and spongy muskeg, on higher ground the mounds and hummocks of caribou moss and tangles of heather that made up the tundra. I headed for a ridge of gravel studded with huge boulders, settled in the lee of one to watch. I could see the lake, and could watch the canoes chasing another band of caribou. On all sides was space, thousands of miles of it reaching into the north, the twisted and gnarled little spruces of the Taiga marching up the slopes.

There was a movement below me, and three caribou appeared in a narrow gully leading to my resting place among the rocks. The wind was in my favor and I froze, waiting. The first was a beautiful bull with an enormous rack; the others, cows. Then I saw the orange ribbons hanging from their ears and somehow for me the sense of the old north was gone. No longer were they of the ancient tundra, of the days of arrows and spears. These animals were managed, part of a scientific research project, specimens in the laboratory of their range.

I felt much the same as when I found a band on a wild mallard I had shot, watched ducklings which had been colored by injections of dye into the eggs from which they came, or saw a grizzly in the mountains of the west with an orange spot on its rump and a transistor inside. Must this, I thought, be the fate of all wild creatures left to us; must we in our need of knowledge mark and record the movements of all free, living things to learn their secrets? Had we now reached a point in our conquest of the earth when, because of our expanding population and human depredations, there was no longer an opportunity for other forms to live undisturbed?

I knew the answers as far as caribou were concerned, knew if they were to survive in the face of what was happening all over the north, much more must be known about them. But at the same time I was saddened to realize that the animals before me had known the hand of man, and was filled with remorse that in our mistreatment of wildlife such measures were necessary to save it from extinction.

The caribou were now within thirty feet, feeding on lichens, moving from patch to patch, nibbling a little from each. Constant movement was the answer to overgrazing, imperative to the continuance of the lichens, herbaceous plants, and willows on which they fed. At the tiny sound of my shutter, they were off with the smooth-gaited stride for which they are famous; and I heard the clicking of their hooves as they ran over the stony slope.

I left my protecting boulder and climbed higher to where I could see the whole of Nejanilini below me. The boats were out again, dashing like silver beetles over the sparkling surface. The winds were at their height and spray flew high, a good day for the tagging crew.

A well-beaten trail led up a draw. It was worn to the gravel, and alongside were whitened antlers and skulls from killings of the past. On one side was a trickle of a spring. The moss was emerald, the willows shoulder high. Flowers bloomed there during the summer and I could see their withered tops. A side trail ran to the spring which seeped out in a steady flow from the gravel of the ridge. I knelt and drank deeply. The water was ice cold and clear. How green that little gully, how different from the dry and stony ridge. Little wonder the caribou made their path there.

I followed the route above the spring into a patch of dwarf spruce where the trail fanned out and the mosses and earth were pawed everywhere. In crossing a swale of golden grass and sedge, I flushed some ptarmigan still in summer's brown and white. The cock soared up with a wild cackle that all but unnerved me, followed by the hen with half a dozen well-grown chicks. They had been feeding on berries and seeds and on the still-tender shoots of green near the sod. The hen returned shortly, did her best to draw me away, fluttered and clucked and dragged a wing, circling nervously.

178

Beyond, I found myself on another open hillside. Here I met a porcupine waddling its way, unconcernedly, from one clump of spruce to another. As I caught up, it stopped, sat on its haunches watching me gravely.

"Hello," I said, "you're a long way from home up here in the Taiga. Better not get too far out on that tundra or you'll be in trouble."

Its black, unblinking eyes surveyed me for a long time, then it moved on, its quill-covered tail wagging from side to side. Exactly like the porky that had girdled one of my red pines back in the Quetico-Superior, the same movement and defensive motion, it was like meeting someone from home. For that matter, many old friends were around me: Labrador tea, Andromeda, bearberry, cotton grass, and caribou moss; and again came the sense I have known many times in the far north, of merely being on an extension of country I knew. As if to convince me this was true, a flock of snow buntings, twittering merrily, flew over and lit in a patch of sedge nearby. Soon I would see their familiar tan and white again wheeling in formation over the weeds in some drifted field far to the south.

On the very summit of the hill I stopped to rest. This, I thought, is how the great plains must have looked to those seeing them for the first time during the migration to the Pacific, the same limitless expanse and sea of space. There was the heavy, matted sod of centuries, cottonwoods in the bottoms of slow, meandering streams, millions of buffalo, antelope, and elk. Here was muskeg, tundra, and caribou, and under it all the permafrost that determined what might live.

I crossed a creek below the ridge and climbed a sandy esker winding across the country, a low embankment of stratified sand and gravel that seemed like a roadway, so smooth was its surface, so well shaped its curves. It looked as new as though the glacier had left only a short time before. To the south, where it is estimated the ice retreated some ten thousand years ago, all such formations are eroded and grown with trees, but on the barrens, these dry river beds that once ran under the glaciers are as distinct as when first exposed. Here, there is little rain and, due to the permafrost, slight run-off and erosion. As a result the eskers and glacial moraines lie almost unchanged.

I found an Indian grave, the carved fence around it down, a weather-worn paddle across it. From this high and lonely place the spirit of the departed could survey the old hunting grounds, watch caribou as long lines wound over the hills, listen to their footsteps as they crossed the stony ridges. In those days, for the grave was very old, the lines of caribou reached from horizon to horizon, and the wolves followed them, while hunters lay in wait; and still the caribou came, and there was always plenty of food.

Gerry Malaher told me a story of another esker grave he had found close to Nejanilini some years before, the first time he and Joe Robertson had come to Duck Lake. Not fifty feet from where they landed they found a fine *ahtikanagan*, or papoose carrier. It was beautifully made and embroidered with bead work and colored cloth, not the sort of thing that would be abandoned without cause, Indians being far too frugal to leave anything so valuable behind. They were curious so followed a trail leading inland to an esker paralleling the shore and there in a slight dip of the formation found an Indian graveyard carefully fenced with spruce stakes. Most of the graves were old, but the head stake of one of them was relatively new.

Several caribou were now in evidence, two in one group, five in another. They grazed around me and when they caught my scent, began to run. Two bulls with enormous antlers held far back on their shoulders, moved into a thicket of spruce. They seemed very dark as they came nearer, their ruffs and flanks startlingly white. I circled, came up against the wind, finally was close and had I been an Indian with a bow or spear, I might have killed one with ease.

Before me now was the outlet of Nejanilini, a river called the Wolverine, the route to the Seal and to the Bay above Fort Churchill. Here are foaming cascades and rapids whose waters are alive with grayling and huge trout. I followed the river for a while looking into its pools and backwaters, hoping to surprise a bear, a fox, or even a wolverine, saw nothing but an osprey soaring high above the channel. The wind was now blowing a gale, the clouds dark and ominous, and it began to rain, a cold sleeting drizzle that drove me into the protection of a dense tangle of spruce against the bank. I found dry branches, kindled a fire and waited out the storm.

After I was warm and dry, I started back over the hills toward camp. The muskeg in the low places was soggy now, the brush dripping, so I followed ridges wherever I could. The wind was bitter and I leaned into it. Gone was the sparkle and glitter of morning, the blue of distant Nejanilini, the singing of birds. I stopped on one of the highest points and looked to the north.

In the space of a few hours, fall had disappeared and the once bright horizons were lost in swirling mist and sleet. I knew now why the caribou came into the Taiga ahead of the storms. Here in these scrubby, moss-hung windbreaks, they would band together for protection, and were I a native, this too would be my wintering place, close to the rapids and its fish, close to the caribou, and out of the wind. Some day I should return, and stay the winter through, for only then could I learn the meanings of this vast and lonely land.

CHAPTER 16

FOND DU LAC

Fond du lac means the end of a waterway, a *voyageur*'s term, usually a place where a river flows in or out of a lake. I know a Fond du lac on Lake Superior where the St. Louis empties into waters from the north; another on Lake Winnebago in Wisconsin; a third far to the northwest between Lake Athabasca and the Wollaston, a river that should have been a major fur-trading route but, because of many rapids and shallows, was never popular. David Thompson, the great map-maker (Mr. Astronomer Thompson, as he was known to the Northwest and to the Hudson's Bay Companies), dreamed of using it as a short cut to far-off Fort Chipewyan where Athabasca meets the Slave on its way to the Mackenzie, but this was not to be. His exploration in 1796 was fraught with so many misadventures that only one official expedition followed—when J. B. Tyrrell of the Canadian Geological Survey traveled the route a century later.

The records of the past century therefore shed scant light on what the river was like. When little is known about an area, legendry and imagination have a habit of filling in the gaps. So it was with the Fond du lac we proposed to follow from the height of land west of Reindeer and Wollaston to the head of Lake Athabasca.

As we prepared to leave Winnipeg, we heard the first of these stories from an old-timer who claimed to have been close to the country during his prospecting and trapping days.

"The rapids up there are terrible," he told us, "no, they're worse than that, absolutely horrible, and no canoes can run them. The portages were given up so long ago, there isn't a trace of them anywhere; no choice but to shoot—or hack your way through."

Another said: "I have heard the Fond du lac is bad to travel, but the flies are what get a man down. There is no place in the whole north including the tundra, where they're as bad—black flies, bull dogs, deer flies, mosquitoes. They're really something and I've seen them pretty rough."

We had excellent aerial surveys, and while few white men had actually been on the ground, our maps were reliable and made us wonder at the authenticity of all legends, especially

184

one—more fantastic than the rest—that had the Fond du lac disappearing into the ground.

"There's one place on that river," an Indian is supposed to have said, "where it goes down into a big hole. None of our people ever go there. It is a spirit place where a Manito lives."

When we reached the end of Wollaston, some ninety miles of open lake with island mirages lying everywhere, we were somewhat curious and not a little apprehensive. Surely, we thought, there must be some basis for these tales, some good reason why no Indians lived there any more. The outlet bay was very pronounced and as we approached there was evidence of flow into the mouth of the river. We were totally unprepared, however, for our first view of the Fond du lac. The bay narrowed sharply and, as we neared, we saw thousands of huge boulders like a wall across the opening of the river. The closer we came, the thicker grew the rocks; and we could see nothing but a great unbroken field of them, with pools of water in between.

We paddled along the edge, but nowhere was space wide enough to take a canoe. If this were the mouth of the Fond du lac, it was almost dry; and if this first rapids were typical, we would have rough going indeed. I climbed out on one of the larger rocks and looked down the river. As far as the first bend, there was no open water in sight but, where the river began to swing, there seemed to be a lead. We might traverse the boulder field, but what lay ahead? Was that sliver of blue water ahead continuous, or were the channels dry? Would we have to portage for miles down a dry stream bed, spend several weeks of back-breaking work instead of one in covering the one-hundred-and-fifty-odd miles to Stony Rapids Post? Perhaps the dour predictions we had heard were not fantasy after all. If the beginning were an indication of what the rest would be, the best thing to do was retrace our steps, go back to Reindeer the way we had come. No party relishes retracing a route and admitting defeat, and never in our experience had we been forced to do so. We all decided to cross the boulders, see what it was like beyond, and if there were any chance at all, to go on if it took until freezeup.

We tried separate channels through the boulders, probed and retreated, dragged the canoes over the rocks, only to return, eventually deciding there was no way but to portage. Between the boulders was water from two to six feet deep, but none of it continuous. In desperation, we unloaded, shouldered the packs, and began jumping from rock to rock. Many of them were slippery and we fell between, but finally the whole outfit was across and piled up safely close to the lead of the open water which, to our joy, seemed to go beyond the bend. Now came the canoes, an entirely different matter. Carrying one on a portage trail is simple, but getting from boulder to boulder is something else. All the time I kept thinking, "if this kind of portaging is ahead, what will happen to the canoes, our outfit, to legs and ankles, should we slip and fall with heavy loads?"

After a couple of hours the canoes were also across and loaded. There was no question anymore of returning and going back down the Blondeau, the Swan, and Reindeer's hundred mile stretch to the south. We were now determined to go on and take whatever came.

We ran two small rapids in succession on our way to Hatchet Lake. They, too, were full of boulders but at least there were channels of deep water and we had no difficulty. David Thompson, in coming up stream from Black Lake, must have been just as happy at finding the river in good flow, for he said in his diary:

"The River had now increased it's water by the addition of the Porcupine and Trout Rivers, and several Brooks; it had also a greater descent; In it's course of One hundred and fifty three miles from the above place of observation in the Black Lake, it meets with and forms many small Lakes; and collects their waters to form a stream of about one, to two, hundred yards in width; it's bottom is sand and pebbles, or rude stones and small rocks, smoothed by the water; on a bed of Limestone, which is the rock of the country; its course is sinuous, from the many hills it meets, and runs around in it's passage; its current is strong, with many rapids, some of them a mile in length: it has four falls. Three of these are about half way down the River; the fourth fall is at the end of a series of rapids, cutting through a high hill; at length the banks become perpendicular, and the river falls eight feet, the carrying place is six hundred yards in length."

We came to know the Fond du lac's rapids and enjoyed them, for none was impassable, the boulders cushioned by enough water so that when we hurtled toward them we rode the swirl and were carried past without touching. We felt as we had on the Sturgeon Weir when leaving the Churchill far to the south, a sense of slaloming as a skier does, sweeping from one stretch of white water to another with the assurance there was always a way through. We portaged around the falls but ran most of the fast water. So confident did we become that, rather than worry about rocks, we watched for grayling leaping ahead of the canoes. Whenever they seemed particularly active, we landed below, broke out the fly rods and began to cast.

I have seen many grayling but never any so completely exciting in their taking of a fly. It may have been the fact they were really hungry, but they rose clear of the water, sometimes several feet, to take the fly on the way down. As soon as the nose of a fish was close, a twitch of the rod tip and it was on. Almost every cast brought a fish, beautiful ones in those clear, cold waters, sixteen to twenty inches in length, weighing up to two-and-a-half pounds, their chief glory the great iridescent dorsal fin with its bright orange border. We kept only enough for a meal ahead, lost track of how many were landed and released. Once, watching a grayling, we narrowly missed a sharp ledge and disaster.

We now knew Thompson's diary by heart and, with the river completely navigable, no longer had any fear. Rapids after rapids disappeared behind us and, where there was any doubt, we waded the shallows and lined the canoes down rather than portage. We had left that great outpouring of granite, schist, and basalt that is known all over the north as the Canadian Shield and were now traveling through a sedimentary formation of limestone. The banks had been carved into caves, canyons, and strangely sculptured battlements where the soft and relatively soluble ledges had been subject to the erosion of the river.

Coming around a sharp bend where the water was very fast, we were watching a particularly interesting cavern. The canoe was moving swiftly, no more than twenty feet from shore. Suddenly, out of the cave stepped a magnificent wolf. It was yellowish white with a distinct ruff of black over its shoulders. For a long moment it stood there, as though aware of the tableau it made, then loped off leisurely along the bank onto a sandspit and was lost to sight. We landed just beyond, and there were its tracks leading across and toward the south. Patches of crowberry and signs of feeding ravens were everywhere, their droppings splashes of purple on rocks and driftwood.

The wolf was the first we had seen on the trip and I was thrilled, for more than any other animal in the north, it is the epitome of wilderness. I can still see its smooth loose-jointed movement, almost a flowing of muscle and sinew.

One night we camped on a high ledge of limestone from which we had a view of the river for miles to the west. So steep was the approach, we were forced to get our water by dropping a bucket on a line into the river. Such a campsite one dreams about, a rushing river below, a view into the sunset, tremendous rock formations on either side. If this, I thought, should ever become a national park, the scene might become world famous. Not as spectacular as Yellowstone, Yosemite, or Jasper, it had a wild, untouched beauty and character of its own. To think we were some of the few who had actually seen it in over a century of time!

The west reddened and, as we sat there in the glow, a moose came out from shore half a mile away; a bull with a great spread of antlers, it walked majestically into the shallows and began wading across, slashing the color as it advanced. On a long sand bar in the very center of the river it stopped, head held high, then splashed through the sunset glow until it disappeared in the timber of the opposite bank.

The following day we passed the place where David Thompson came to grief. After many rapids and stretches of fast water, so many we lost count, the river dropped over a series of ledges impossible to run or avoid. We landed well above, looked for a portage and found it on the left side, a trail that skirted a clump of birches close to the water's edge. Here the great map-maker almost lost his life.

"On our return," he states in his diary, "and about half way up the black river [the Fond du lac], we came to one of the falls, with a strong rapid both above and below it, we had a carrying place of 200 yards, we then attempted the strong current above the fall, they were to track the canoe up by a line, walking on shore, while I steered it, when they had proceeded about eighty yards, they came to a birch tree, growing at the edge of the water, and there stood and disputed between themselves on which side of the tree the tracking line should pass. I called to them to go on, they could not hear me for the noise of the fall, I then waved my hand for them to proceed, meanwhile the current was drifting me out, and having only one hand to guide the canoe, the Indians standing still, the canoe took a sheer across the current, to prevent the canoe upsetting, I waved my hand to them to let go the line and leave me to my fate, which they obeyed. I sprang to the bow of the canoe took out my clasp knife, cut the line from the canoe and put the knife in my pocket, by this time I was on the head of the fall, all I could do was to place the canoe to go down bow foremost, in an instant the canoe was precipitated down the fall and buried under the waves, I was struck out of the canoe and when I arose among the waves, the canoe came on me and buried beneath it, to raise myself I struck my feet against the rough bottom and came up close to the canoe which I grasped and being now in shoal water, I was able to conduct the canoe to the shore."

According to his diary he lost almost everything:

"nothing remained in the canoe but an ax, a small tent of grey cotton, and my gun: also a pewter basin. When the canoe was hauled on shore I had to lay down on the rocks, wounded, bruised, and exhausted by my exertions."

The Indians had run down along the shore and returned with the precious cork-lined box containing his sextant and a few instruments, the papers of his survey, and maps. All Thompson had left was his shirt and a thin, linen vest. His companions had also lost everything they owned, so for protection and warmth they cut the tent into three pieces to wrap around themselves as a defense against flies and the cold at night.

As Thompson rose from the rocks where he lay, he found blood on his left foot and saw that the flesh, from the heel almost to the toes, had been torn away when he struck his feet against the bottom. The Indians bound his foot with part of the tent, and helped him to stand. Unassisted he walked over the carrying place with its "rude stones and banks."

The Indians went into the woods to find gum to patch the badly broken canoe, but they were confronted with the problem of starting a fire because they had lost their firesteel and flint. Thompson took the flint from the one remaining gun and when he drew out his knife from his pocket, to use the steel, he said it was "as though I had drawn a ghost out of my pocket and I heard them whisper to each other, how avaricious a white man must be, who rushing on death takes care of his little knife."

"I said to them, if I had not saved my little knife, how could we make a fire, you fools go to the Birch Trees and get some touch wood which they soon brought, a fire was made, we repaired our canoe and carried all above the Fall and the Rapid, they carried the canoe, my share was the gun, axe, and pewter basin; and Sextant Box. Late in the evening we made a fire and warmed ourselves. It was now our destitute condition that stared us in the face, a long journey through barren country, without provisions or the means of obtaining any, almost naked, and suffering from the weather, all before us was very dark, but I had hopes that the Supreme Being through our Great Redeemer to whom I made short prayers morning and evening would find some way to preserve us; on the second day, in the afternoon we came on a small lake of the river and in a grassy bay we saw two large Gulls hovering, this lead us to think they were taking care of their young, we went and found three young gulls, which we put in the canoe, it may be remarked the Gull cannot dive, he is too light; these gulls gave us but little meat. They had not four ounces of meat on them. It appeared to sharpen hunger."

The next day they found an eagle's nest some sixteen feet above the ground in the spreading branches of a birch tree. The Indian, Kozdah, was sent to rob the nest, but in the midst of his depredations, the old ones arrived and Thompson and the other Indian pelted them with stones and shouted until the young were thrown out of the nest onto the ground. Kozdah picked up one of them, but the young bird drove its talons so deeply into his wrist, Thompson was forced to cut the foot from the body before it was released.

They cleaned and roasted the birds and during the night awoke in the throes of violent dysentery. Thompson made a strong brew of Labrador tea which helped them recover. Day after day from then on they lived on crowberries, which are not nutritious and sometimes even poisonous, until, as Thompson said, "Both Paddy [the other Indian] and myself were now like skeletons, effects of hunger, dysentery, from cold nights, and so weak, that we thought it useless to go any further but die where we were."

Kozdah was in much better shape than his companions for he had known the danger of eating the fat of young eagles, had therefore avoided the entrails and had escaped the aftermath of dysentery. His conscience began to bother him for not warning the others and he was concerned for fear they might perish and he be blamed. Neither Thompson nor Paddy suspected the truth when Kozdah's morale began to weaken.

"Kozdah," wrote Thompson, "now burst into tears, upon which we told him that he was yet strong as he had not suffered from the disease. He replied, if both of you die, I am sure to be killed for everyone will believe I have killed you both, the white men will revenge your death on me and the Indians will do the same for him; I told him then to get some thin white birch rind, and I would give him a writing, when he did, with charcoal, I then wrote a short account of our situation, which I gave him upon which he said now I am safe."

Finally the starving and desperate men met with a party of Chipewyans who gave them food, flint and steel, a pair of shoes, and a kettle, after which Thompson wrote:

"We now proceeded on our journey with thanks to God and cheerful hearts and without any accident on the 21st of July arrived at Fairford House from whence we commenced our journey. From this time to the 26th of August, our time was spent in fishing and hunting, and with all our exertions could barely maintain ourselves."

As we sat on our campsite that night listening to the roar of the river below, Thompson was very much with us. Though he had been there over a century and a half before, it could have happened yesterday, so little had the country changed. During the day we had seen several eagles, as well as gulls and ducks, but outside of the wolf, the moose, and one caribou several days back, had seen no game. We were on the Fond du lac almost a month later than Thompson which accounted for the lack of flies, and he was coming upstream when he wrote his account, while we were going down.

What interested me most in his diary was how the character of the great map-maker emerged during his time of crisis. Why he told Kozdah and Paddy to cast him loose and then cut his tracking line, I do not know, but taking the time while plunging over the falls to place his knife back into his pocket was typical of the man. In the face of death, he did the customary, routine thing. His was a mind that brooked no deviation, and he showed here the indomitable will and courage that had carried him all over the northwest.

When we approached Manito Falls, we realized it must be the place where the river was supposed to disappear. From both Thompson's and Tyrrell's accounts we knew it could be no other, and that unless some recent geological catastrophe had taken place, there was nothing to the story we had heard. Nevertheless, we were curious, knowing from past experience that there must be some basis for such a legend. As we neared, the river narrowed, the banks grew more precipitous, and we could hear a roar ahead and see spray and mist over the trees. Rounding a bend, we saw a quarter of a mile away the hole through which the river supposedly plunged.

This evidently was the turning point beyond which Indians would not go. We beached the canoes and climbed the bank; from there it seemed as though the river actually did go down into a gigantic opening. We studied the spot and quickly found the reason. At this place the river made a sharp, almost right-angled turn, so sharp that even from a height it could not be seen to continue. The rocks on either side were deeply eroded and, from where we stood, it looked as though the river went down between the banks. Into the canoes once more, we approached warily. The current grew stronger. We hugged the shore. Just before the bend, we landed on a flat shelf and climbed a ridge. From a high rock we could see the river beyond. It did not disappear!—it was merely lost to view as it plunged between the steep limestone walls of what had looked like a cavern.

Thompson described it graphically:

"For half a mile further the current is very swift; it is then for one hundred and eighteen yards, compressed in a narrow channel of rock only twelve yards in width. At the end of this channel a bold perpendicular-sided point of limestone rock projects at right angles to the course of the river, against which the rapid current rushes and appears driven back with such force that the whole river seems as if turned up from its bottom. It boils, foams and every drop is white; part of the water is driven down a precipice of twenty feet descent; the greater part rushes through the point of rock and disappears for two hundred yards; then issues out in boiling whirlpools. The dashing of the water against the rocks, the deep roar of the torrent, the hollow sound of the fall, with the surrounding high, frowning hills form a scenery grand and awful, and it is well named the Manito Fall. While the Nahathaways possessed the country, they made offerings to it, and thought it the residence of a Manito; they have retired to milder climates; and the Chipewyans have taken their place who make no offerings to anything; but my companions were so awe struck, that the one gave a ring, and the other a bit of tobacco. They heard of this Fall, but never saw it before."

It was midafternoon so decided to pitch our camp near the falls. We found a good place for the tents back from the water's edge, and a cooking spot on a flat ledge in full view of the river's awesome drop into the gorge below. A sea gull sat quietly on a point of rock to one side of the falls. Every so often it would take off to circle the swirl below, usually picking up a small fish before returning to its perch. Time and again it did this, merely spreading its wings and floating down below to search the foam-laced whirlpools. No doubt some gull had sat there when Thompson with his two companions Paddy and Kozdah came through.

After camp was pitched and supper out of the way, we walked around and surveyed our site. Growing over the rocks was a finely leaved heather I had not seen before, possibly a sub-arctic species of Labrador tea. The flowers were gone, but color was beginning to show everywhere. Most of the evening we sat and looked at the falls and listened to its roar, and that night went to sleep with the air full of its thunder.

In the morning we made the portage and pushed down the current. As we rounded the first bend, the sound of Manito Falls was gone and with it the legend of the river that disappeared and all the fearsome stories we had heard. If legends are runes, we had run them down; if runes are truths, feelings, and mysteries, we had found them on the Fond du lac, but more than that was our sense of having traveled with a great explorer, Mr. Astronomer Thompson, and of having known the joys and hazards that were his on this forgotten and seldom-used route of the past.

CHAPTER 17

THE DIVIDE

For two hundred miles, we had
followed the mighty Churchill east to South Indian. Now we
must change our direction and go south to the Burntwood
River in order to reach Nelson House. Between the Churchill
and the Burntwood is the Rat River, a relatively untraveled
stream which almost connects the two drainages. To reach it
we were forced to leave our major waterway and cross a
divide.

In the three-thousand-odd miles of the old Voyageur's
Highway, from Montreal to Fort Chipewyan in the far northwest, are four major divides and many minor ones. Sometimes

portages are very short or as long as the Methye of thirteen miles between the Churchill and the Mackenzie valley. Headwaters often originate in swamps or in labyrinths of tiny, twisting creeks; but whatever the situation, leaving one watershed and crossing a divide to another, in the old days of the trade was considered a momentous occasion and worthy of a celebration.

One of the most famous divides is the Height of Land Portage west of Lake Superior, the ridgepole of the continent where waters run south into the Great Lakes and east to the Atlantic, west through the Rainy River system, and north to Hudson Bay, while a short distance away is the drainage to the Mississippi and the Gulf of Mexico. *Voyageurs* crossing this divide between North and South Lakes were formally baptised to become true *hommes du nord*. Until a man made this portage, he was merely an ordinary *mangeur du lard*, or pork-eater from Montreal; but afterward, he was a Northwester, entitled to wear a feather in his cap. It was the dream of every *voyageur* who had ever swung a paddle or packed a load, to earn this distinction. Through this baptism he grew in stature for it meant he had proved his mettle and worth and could boast with the best of them to the end of his days.

Alexander Henry states in his diary: "At this place the men generally finish their small kegs of liquor and fight many a battle." But the best account is in the description of another early trader, John Macdonell:

"Passed the Martes, les Perches (portages) and slept at the

height of Land, where I was instituted a North Man by Baptême, performed by sprinkling water in my face with a small cedar Bow dipped in a ditch of water and accepting certain conditions such as not to let any new hand pass by that road without experiencing the same ceremony which stipulated particularly never to kiss a voyageur's wife against her own free will, the whole being accompanied by a dozen of Gun shots fired one after the other in an Indian manner. The intention of this Baptême, being only to claim a glass, I complied with the custom and gave the men,—a two gallon keg as my worthy Bourgeois Mr. Cuthbert Grant directed me."

As we approached the divide which separated us from the Rat, we shared the feelings of the old *voyageurs*, for there is something psychological in passing from one watershed to another. Somehow, when following a stream, one moves with the flow, not only physically but mentally. It is almost as though one's lines of force were oriented with those of a major gravitational field. All thoughts lead a certain way; one becomes easterly thinking, northerly, or westerly, so to change direction suddenly as we were now to do, seemed a violation of all our previous orientation. At South Indian Post, some ten miles from our portage into the Rat, we felt this coming on and while we welcomed the challenge, it disturbed us, for we knew once we left the east-flowing river, with its big lakes and open terrain, and turned south, travel would be entirely different. While our maps showed something of the character of the area, we were totally unprepared for what lay ahead. Questioning the natives at the post was not reassuring and merely served to make us even more uncertain of our immediate future.

"The Rat," laughed an old man, "bad, very bad, water so deep," and he held up four fingers, "walk, walk, walk, walk, pull canoe through grass, much brush and logs."

"When were you there?" I asked.

"Long time ago, many years, I guess."

"Any Indians go that way now?" I asked another.

"No Indians go any more," was the reply, "too hard, better long portage to Costello."

One Indian said he had trapped in the region some time ago, but all we got from him was a reaffirmation of the story that the upper Rat was bad and should not be followed except on urgent business.

We left the trading post late in the afternoon and headed toward the Rat. The lake was as we had known it for days, glassy calm, with reflections everywhere. Terns circled above us and their scree—screee—screeee—seemed everywhere. They wheeled in clouds and, when we approached nesting places, took to the air until the sky was aglitter with silver wings.

Knowing what was coming, we relished those open expanses with their distant blue horizons; so, rounding a last point, we turned for a farewell look. For fifty miles the waterway ran on to where it joined North Indian again, then running eastward for two hundred miles to the Bay. We were leaving the route we had followed over the years from the Mackenzie Divide, almost a thousand miles away, to this turning point on South Indian. We were abandoning its great calms and storms, its vistas, immensities, and roaring rapids for something new and unfamiliar. That night it was decided we must have a camp to remember, one that caught in a final display all the great Churchill had meant to us.

We found our site in a little protected bay from which we could look out to the lake with a view to the west. Several islands lay beyond, their reflections clear. Ducks were overhead constantly, and terns laid siege to our privacy. We pitched our tents, cooked our meal, then sat and watched until dark.

"Fill your mind and your eyes," I kept reminding myself, "try and remember," but strangely enough, somehow we were already over the divide.

In the morning we ate a substantial breakfast, knowing we would need it, packed swiftly, and started for the portage and our battle with the bush. We slipped into a little weedy bay and landed at its very end. Before us and not twenty feet from the water's edge was a smooth ridge so low I could have thrown a pebble across without trying.

"The divide," said Elliot, looking it over, "evidently all there is. Across that little hump is the Rat."

We sat there for a moment surveying the little rise that separated the watershed of the Churchill from the Rat, the Burntwood, and the mighty Nelson. It seemed incongruous, even deflating, after all we had heard. It should have been a mighty divide to fight our way across, a mountain to scale, at least something to test our strength and endurance.

"A blast of dynamite," said Blair, "and the Rat could steal the Churchill, start a flood that would scour out the bed of a new river"—an act of piracy not unknown in geological annals where headwater streams approach each other with the exploring fingers of their origins.

We landed, unloaded the canoes, packed the outfit over the bank to the edge of a marshy pond, and paddled to where a small stream ran out into a dense thicket of alder, scrub spruce, and dwarf birch. We glanced at the outlet with dismay, saw it was absolutely impassable, carried over an old trail where the creek emerged again. No more than ten feet wide, it dove into a leafy tunnel with windfalls and thick brush on either side.

There was just enough water to float the canoes, from a few inches in depth to a foot or two—and I remembered the Indian who had held up his four fingers. Then began the strangest trek any of us had ever made, a plunge down a mill-race barely wide enough to permit our Prospectors to go through, turns so sharp it was impossible to make some of them without backing up, the current so strong it hurled us time and again against the banks. Though chopped-out long ago, the cut branches were still razor sharp.

It began to rain, and the tangle of vegetation and debris became a soggy and dripping chute. We were thankful for a bottom of mud and sand and that we could follow the creek without much danger of ripping the canvas of the canoes. Once I lost my hat while ducking low overhanging branches and had to push back to retrieve it. Another time the arm of my wool shirt was impaled on a spike and ripped badly. Going through such a maze we had to guard our eyes and faces with our arms, trusting to luck we would go the right way. The dim light, the rain, the countless bends, made our progress slow and interminable; and we wondered how much longer it could go on.

After several hours, we lost track of the others; and while we knew Eric and Elliot, Blair and Omond, were ahead, Tony and I felt utterly alone. Finally the creek widened, fanned-out into a vast marsh of rushes and horsetail, losing itself in what seemed an endless sea of green. Somewhere ahead, according to our maps, was Lake Issett, but where, we could not tell.

Before us was a broad lagoon and we entered it joyfully, sure it was the way. Yellow water lilies grew in profusion and beds of pickerel weed lay pink against the green. We pushed down the full length of the opening, found an old beaver dam which indicated a once-flowing channel, went confidently through a narrow break and into a still larger pond. We continued with high hopes, then suddenly the water was stagnant and dead, the creek disappearing entirely in a limitless expanse of bog.

I stood up to look around. For miles there was only swamp.

Eric and Elliot went into what looked like a narrows, got out of their canoe when they could push no farther, began to wade, finally returned. We retraced our steps back through the broken beaver dam and into the first lagoon, took a lead west, looking for signs of current, watching the grass for the slightest telltale leaning that might indicate any movement of water. The rushes grew denser and denser until only with the greatest effort could we force our way forward. At last the three canoes were high and dry on a solid mass of vegetation. To the west a mile away appeared to be a shore line of spruce and birch, possibly only an esker, with the great marsh surrounding it on all sides. Ahead was a little hummock, a tiny island of rock protruding from the bog.

"Tony," I said, "I'm going to get out, wade through the muck, climb to the top of that island, and see what's ahead."

"We'll wait here," he replied. "Good Luck."

I stepped over the side, sloshed ahead to the rock, climbed it, looked in every direction, then, toward the distant shore-line, I saw a thin streak of blue.

"Water," I yelled, "water to the west."

From then on we fought our way, ankle deep, sometimes to our hips, through mud and grass. Again the terns screeing above us, and ducks constantly on the wing. Eventually we reached a point too deep to wade, with just enough water to float the canoes, and we poled until we could actually paddle. Now the rushes did lean forward. We were in a channel and before us at last was Issett Lake.

We made camp on a little point at dusk. Six loons coasted in the open, calling constantly. We were the first to enter their marshy sanctuary in years and deserved the wild welcome they gave us. Wet from wading and the rain, we built a big fire to dry out and then cooked supper. This was real wilderness, off the beaten trail; and, as far as we knew, none of the old explorers had come through here. True back country it was, unknown and unwanted even by the Indians.

The Rat, according to our maps, should have more volume now due to entering streams, and below was a chain of lakes with such strange, unpronounceable names as Karsakuwigamak, Pemichigamaw, Rat, Misinagu, Notigo, and Wapisu—names known to very few. The next morning the little lake was covered with mist and we could see only a few hundred yards. As it lifted, phantom islands emerged, gradually the shores appeared, and soon we could see the outlet to the south.

We paddled into the bay and found a channel like a canal, the flow steady, water again covered with yellow lilies. The banks of mud and clay were grown with grass and scattered clumps of spruce. In places where the current quickened, we watched carefully for hidden rocks. This was no time to take a chance on ripping out the bottom of a canoe. Again the rain, and at noon we stopped at an abandoned trapper's cabin and built a fire to dry out. The shelter had not been occupied for a long time and the clearing where it stood was ablaze with fireweed. Whoever had used it must have come, we decided, from Nelson House, rather than over the difficult route we had used.

The river became larger and larger and some of the lakes through which we passed were beautiful, narrow winding channels with rocky shores and such high skylines it seemed at times as though we were paddling through spruce-pinnacled canyons. One night we camped on Karsakuwigamak, meaning narrow, winding lake, as charming a body of water as we had ever known, on another night at Rat Lake itself—and in their beauty and solitude forgot the swampy country we had struggled through to get there.

It was below Rat Lake that we ran into burns for the first time. All morning we had traversed one gorgeous channel after another and were convinced that the Rat River system was one of the finest in the whole north. So impressed were we with its stands of tall, slender spruce marching up the rocky slopes, it was a shock suddenly to come to a place where trees lay in great brown windrows. One moment the skyline of spruce was untouched, the next it was gone; the rocks sat naked and exposed where once they had been cushioned with moss, lichens, and herbaceous growth. A ground fire creeping through the duff had consumed the shallow bed of humus over the rocks. With their rootholds gone, the trees fell every which way, one on top of another in great and tangled confusion. Had it not been for the ash and charred roots, I might have believed a tornado had done the damage, as I had once seen a field of ripe wheat flattened by wind and rain.

We paddled close and saw water seeping down the bare surfaces of granite rock—little trickles, broad thin sheets of it, rivulets in the gullies—every slope shining with moisture.

"The shores are bleeding," said Tony, "losing their life's blood."

This was the truth. No longer able to hold moisture, waters that once were held by the accumulated humus and moss were now carrying the decay of centuries into the waters of the lake. It would take a long time for those shores to come back. While some trees might grow in the depressions, the open faces of rock would become more and more naked until they looked as they were when the glacier left.

We discovered many recent burns along the Rat, some having leapt from shore to shore in the narrows, and we passed bleeding banks for many miles. With the precious moss gone, there was no foothold for the trees and shrubs that provided food for birds, insects, and mammals. The forest would return eventually, but should the fire come again into the tinder-dry maze of resin-soaked spruce, everything would burn to the rocks with nothing left but gray ash. Rains and melting snows would wash even that away until the bare, white bones of the land lay exposed. Then recovery would take centuries.

Eventually we left the burns and late one afternoon came to a rapids none of us considered running. We had shot a number on the way, none difficult compared to those of the Churchill, but this one looked impossible; so we carried to an old Indian camp at the far end where a smooth ledge of rock lay parallel to the river.

Our tents were pitched back in an opening the Indians had used, but mine was near the rapids, for that night I wanted to sleep close to the sound of the water. After camp was finished, Omond got out his rod to see if we might get some walleyes for supper. With the very first cast, he hooked a four-pounder, a beautiful fish, well-colored and firm in flesh. I seized it with delight, filleted it immediately. Blair, Tony, and Elliot then came down and it was the same with them, almost every cast a splendid pike. Within a short time we had over a dozen and I was kept busy stripping off fillets until not only did we have enough for supper, but for breakfast as well.

With the fishing over, Omond busied himself with a special concoction of rum to celebrate as *voyageurs* should, our conquering of the Rat. He laid out cups on the shelf of rock beside the river while I sliced a supply of thin strips from the fillets and fried them golden crisp. The shelf itself had a backrest along its full length and here the *voyageurs* ensconced themselves in an expectant row. Omond served the rum and I passed along a heaping platter of hot fillet strips. Never had anything tasted quite so good. Half an hour before, those tidbits had been swimming in the rapids.

"To the Rat," said Tony, "to the miserable Rat, the horse-tail swamp."

"And to the finest campsite we've ever had," added Eric.

"We've earned this one. Anyone coming here is entitled to luxury."

And this was true, no one would ever come here without cause. No planes could fly to this particular spot, no quick expeditions without portaging or paddling. We had earned the right to be there, and sat on the ledge and savored our triumph to the utmost—the white seething river before us, the swirls so full of fish we could have taken a hundred. This was a place to remember and cherish; it was worth all the battling to get there.

We rolled-in early and went to sleep to the sound of roaring water. During the night I awakened, opened the mosquito bar and looked out. The river was full of surging mist, the air drenched with the smell of mint, for near the ledge was a bed of it that had been trampled and crushed. A sliver of moon hung overhead, just enough to lighten the rapids. To the north was a hint of the aurora, no flaming this time, no great zigzag curtains, merely a brightening of the sky. For a long time I lay with my head outside the bar, smelling the almost overpowering fragrance, looking into the mysterious plunge of misty water and listening to the rush of it. In the morning we would continue down the river, with luck find another good camp, then Three Point Lake and the entrance to the Burntwood below Nelson House.

The following day we traversed the last of the Rat, now grown to a sizeable river. The weather was clear and a fair wind pushed us along. The horizon was hazy toward Nelson, so we knew there were active fires ahead. At times smoke billowed high in surging clouds of brown and white where it raced through crowns of spruce. We were lucky to be in big, open country again, and not on a small stream whose portages were crisscrossed with charred windfalls, and ankle deep in smoking ash.

That night we stopped on a little lake known as Wapisu, the end of the Rat River chain, at a narrows with a view to the west. On either side were rushes and, as we made camp, flocks of teal, scaup, and mallards flew by.

"What a spot for decoys," said Elliot, "you could sit here all day and be sure that whatever came into the lake would pass."

It was close to September and the flocks were beginning to move; all evening we listened to the whisper of their wings. The sun set angrily and, just as we were about to crawl into our sleeping bags, two canoes came along; and, when they saw our fire, the Indians paddled in. There were nine all told, an old man and his wife, teen-age girls and boys, smaller children and two dogs. We held their canoes as they scrambled out and then they sat quietly around the fire. I served them tea, bannock, dried sausage, and some cookies from South Indian Post.

They had come, the old man told us, from Nelson House to do some hunting and fishing up the river, had seen a moose in the bay across, would give us meat if the boys were lucky in the morning.

"Bad trouble at Nelson House," said the old man, "very bad trouble."

"What happened?" I asked, "Anyone hurt or sick?"

"Very bad trouble," he repeated, "woman kill man with stick. Now police come, take her to jail. Got children, very bad."

Not until the end of our trip did we learn the story of the woman who killed a man in defense of her family honor. The stick turned out to be a rather substantial one, a stick of heavy cordwood. What the outcome was and how justice was meted out in the bush we never heard, but knowing the Mounties and their understanding of native codes, I am sure it was just and fair.

We had a good visit and then the canoes disappeared in the dusk toward the bay where they had seen the moose. They would try for their meat at dawn. This was our last camp on the River Rat; in the morning we would be on our way to Nelson, go down the Burntwood with its gorgeous falls and rapids to the railhead at the mining town of Thompson.

CHAPTER 18

RENDEZVOUS ON CONJUROR BAY

WE WERE in a gay mood when we made camp one night on the shores of Conjuror Bay, the entrance to Great Bear. Towering around us were blue, tumbled hills, glaciated mountains rising a thousand feet or more from the water's edge, rock without trees, barren, cold, and lifeless. Under ordinary circumstances we might have been apprehensive, but that night it was as beautiful and exciting as its name. I was extravagant with our food, knowing in the morning we could restock at Eldorado; Omond, just as generous with his carefully guarded store of rum. Another day and our worries would be over.

I like names like Conjuror Bay. The very sound of them speaks of romance, mystery, and challenge. Far places with names like that are goals worth striving for and, when achieved, glow in one's memories. There are many: Compulsion Bay at the lower end of Wollaston, Fort Reliance on Great Slave, Artillery Lake just west of the headwaters of the Thelon, Trafalgar Bay on Northern Light, and Coronation Gulf where the Coppermine flows into the Arctic Sea; names that have color, power, and meaning. When, after fighting gales, running unknown rapids and feeling the breath of the Arctic itself, you finally come to a place like Conjuror Bay, it enters your spirit and gives you a sense of identity with the men whose imaginations bestowed such a heroic title.

Long before the expedition began, we had arranged to be met there by a boat from the radium mine at Echo Bay. Great Bear with its enormous expanse of open water, and with few islands or promontories to break the wind, was a chance we could not take. It was close to freeze-up time; we dared not lose even a day. Snow was already in the air and, with food running short, we would be sorely pressed if forced to fight our way to the mouth of the Great Bear River over 150 miles to the west.

Eldorado was the name of the mine at Echo Bay. Just a few miles south of the Arctic Circle, it was one of the first big radium mines on the continent, had produced ore for the bombs that destroyed Hiroshima and Nagasaki. It had been discovered by prospectors who had noted in the journals of the Canadian Geological Survey that cobalt bloom was in evidence on the shores of Great Bear's Echo Bay, "colors that gave scintillating reflections in deep transparent water." That observation by Dr. J. Mackintosh Bell in 1900 was the key, and when an aerial survey party under the leadership of Gilbert Labine, thirty years later, saw the bloom, it was the beginning of a major development.

"What sort of a craft will pick us up?" I asked Omond.

"Oh," he said, rubbing his whiskers, "possibly an old scow with an outboard run by an Indian."

"I'll wager it will be a big freighter canoe," said Eric, "a twenty-two footer, big enough to take us all with the canoes in tow."

We didn't care what it proved to be, just so we could get over the broad surface of the lake before a storm blew up.

"A hot shower," remarked Blair, "will make a human being out of me."

None of us had had a real bath since we started, with the exception of Eric who went into the water each morning though ice was along the shores. I found a pool one day in which I cleaned a trout. It seemed warmer than the rest of the lake for it was shallow, and that day the sun had shone for almost an hour. There I had my bath, and though I smelled faintly of fish for a while, at least I was fairly clean.

Denis added, "I'll settle for a soft bed, some fresh meat, and a chance to sit in a chair for a while."

Coming out of the bush even for a day or two is a tremendous adventure, almost as great as going in, and here at Conjuror Bay we were happy for our reprieve. We would stay only overnight, and if all went well, ride a scow, a barge, or some kind of craft down the big lake to the mouth of the river we would follow to the Mackenzie.

The following morning we were up early, ate a hurried breakfast, scoured pots and dishes, packed up with an enthusiasm none of us could hide. The rendezvous was for ten o'clock but we were ready early, the canoes in a row down at the water, packs stacked neatly beside them, everything checked and double checked, the campsite cleaned and policed as though for inspection.

Elliot strolled around and looked the situation over with satisfaction, thinking, I knew, of army days when one of his divisions was ready to move.

"This outfit's about to roll," he said, "not a thing out of place. All we need is transport."

"Where do you suppose it will come?" I asked as he glanced at his map.

"Around the headland," he said, pointing to the west, "there's a channel beyond leading to the open lake."

I knew without asking where it would be, and so did all the rest. Ever since our arrival we had known, but someone simply had to ask to relieve the tension. We sat on the rocks, watching and waiting, our eyes on the headland.

At exactly ten, Blair got to his feet.

"Do you suppose the word got through on our rendez-vous?" he asked. "Something might have happened."

"Not a chance," replied Eric, "if they left Eldorado this morning, we'll see them soon."

At ten thirty we were vaguely uneasy. By noon the wind would be up. None of us relished a battle against the icy waves of an open body of water as wide as Lake Superior.

At ten forty-five we heard a strange sound, a sort of hum beyond the hills. It wasn't the wind, but could be an aircraft flying high. We scanned the skies but there was no sign. The drone continued, seemed to die, but then steadied, no closer than before.

"A motor," said Elliot with conviction, "a motor of some kind and on the water."

It did not sound like an outboard, not the hard, raucous roar of an open engine, but rather muffled and subdued. Suddenly it was much louder in the direction of the channel. Then to our amazement a great sea-going ship steamed majestically around the headland, a magnificent craft with cargo cranes, lifeboats, davits, black figures along the rail. We could not believe our eyes.

"An outboard," said Omond, "an old scow."

"The Santa Maria," yelled Tyler from his lookout on a rock.

We were completely surprised and baffled. Such a ship way up in the bush! We stared as though expecting the mirage to disappear, but it bore down swiftly and when it blew three

218

earth-shaking blasts, we knew it was real. Straight on it came and, when it looked as though it must surely ram the shore, reversed engines, and dropped anchor not a hundred feet away.

"Paddle out," yelled the captain, "we'll lift you all aboard."

We threw packs into the canoes, jumped in, and in a moment were alongside. Ropes were fastened fore and aft, winches started, the canoes with all their gear hoisted over the side and lowered gently to the open deck.

Jock McNiven, the superintendent at Eldorado, a bluff and hearty soul with a voice like a foghorn, greeted us jovially and invited us to the galley for pie and coffee.

By the time we were back on deck, the *Radium Gilbert* was moving down the channel and heading up the coast. What a change from riding frail canoes! The headlands of the Bay, while still overpowering, had lost something of their menace, for now we were warm and safe, and in full control once more. Strange, I thought, what the consciousness of steel and power can do to a man's perspective.

In a couple of hours we steamed into Echo Bay and tied up at a dock below the white, sprawling installations of the mine. Jock led us swiftly to the guest house, and had our clothes taken to be washed.

"Don't spare the hot water," he boomed as he left, "we've got enough for two hundred men"; and so we showered and showered until we could take it no longer, dried with great rough towels and rested on bunks that were soft and clean. No one could possibly understand what luxury this was, until he had known days and weeks of bitter cold, hard work, and exposure.

We dressed leisurely in our clean clothes, felt immaculate and spruce, found our way to the mess hall and banqueted on fresh beef and potatoes with gravy, hot rolls, cake, and apple pie, until we could eat no more.

In the afternoon we toured the mine and the plant, saw the veins where raw ore lay and learned how it was crushed and refined through elaborate processes of precipitation and chemical action. Later Jock showed us the bloom which Bell had found on the rocks along the shore, and we heard how, during the war, the mine had worked to capacity. The ship had been brought in by air, by barge, by tractors, and was assembled and welded together at the mine to transport refined ore to the Mackenzie and bring in men, equipment, and supplies from the outside.

The next morning we flew toward the Dismal Lakes north and east of Great Bear, watched the sparse timber of the north shore gradually give way to open tundra. We landed on a little lake known as Lac Rouvière and had lunch over a tiny fire of willow sticks and heather. This was close to the Coppermine and to Coronation Gulf where we had planned to go originally, the route we abandoned in favor of the Camsell when there were rumors of ice all the way to the sea.

After we ate we took off for Coronation Gulf. We wanted

to see the place where the expedition would have ended had we not been warned. Across the divide lay the Coppermine, open in the gorges and rapids, but sheathed in ice where waters slowed. Some tributaries looked white and solid as in early spring. Had we attempted the route, we might have had to abandon canoes and equipment and either follow the river on foot to the sea some five hundred miles away, or go back to our starting point on Great Slave. We flew over the great bend and headed for Bloody Falls, but white fogs rolling in from the Arctic Coast forced us to return before we reached the mountains. The vast tundra now ablaze with autumn color would soon be white with snow.

Back again at Eldorado, warm and well fed, it seemed almost incongruous to think we might have ventured forth by canoe into such bleak and inhospitable terrain as we had seen. For that matter, it was almost as strange to continue our trip, so swiftly had the impact of comfort affected our minds.

The *Radium Gilbert* was waiting for us the following noon, the trip to take the balance of the day, and until noon of the next, before we sighted the mouth of the Great Bear River where we would take to the canoes once more. As we boarded, I looked at our four Prospectors lying amidships, at the pile of packs beside them lashed down with a tarp against a blow. It was hard to realize this was the same familiar outfit we had ridden, portaged, and lived with all the way down the Camsell to the Bear. The feeling would not last for long.

Within twenty-four hours we would know it again as we sped down the eighty-odd miles of the Great Bear River to the Mackenzie.

As we moved out into the open expanses of the lake, I kept saying to myself, "This is Great Bear, this the great blob of blue on the maps just south of the Arctic Coast." After years of planning and dreaming of coming this far north, the actuality was almost an anticlimax. There should have been a burst of cannon fire, a waving of flags, and wild huzzas to mark such a tremendous event, but all I could hear was the soft moan of the great engines, their steady throbbing, and the wash from the bow. As the bold, mountainous shores receded, a mirage took form in the south: clusters of islands and points where we knew there should be none. To the north was the land of Father Rouvière, of Sir John Franklin, and Richard Camsell; in a slight depression, Dease Bay, the outlet of the river from the Dismal Lakes and the route to the Coppermine; to the west, open horizons and space.

The afternoon was cloudless, the shores growing blue in the distance with a chance for a sunset. After supper in the galley, I bedded-down on deck—for I wanted to get the feel of Great Bear, watch the sunset until it was dark and, if awakened, catch perhaps the blaze of northern lights. Two nights in a room were enough. I wanted no walls around me now, only the sound of water and the calling of gulls.

Morning dawned bright and the shores of the west end stood clear. To the right was Fort Franklin and, through the glasses, I could see the usual white building with its red roof, the Hudson's Bay Post, a school, a church with a white spire, cabins strung along the beach. I knew dogs were howling and straining at their leashes as we hove into view. This was the fort established by Sir John Franklin in 1825, a reminder of his ill-fated expedition to the north and the loss of all his men. The fort faded behind us as we approached the narrow bay of the outlet. I remembered then the advice at Eldorado.

"Don't try to run that river without Indian guides. White water all the way down. The Charles Rapids is seven miles long—and rough."

I had read about the Bear, studied it on the maps; over eighty miles in length it ran almost due west, had cut its bed through glacial moraine in one great slash. With a current of ten miles an hour, and many rough spots, anything could happen, and we knew from experience in the far north how cold such waters were and what it would mean if we upset.

"Pick up your guides at Fort Franklin," said our informant, "those Indians know the rocks."

We had never hired guides and would not now. If we could not run the rapids we would line the canoes down or portage as we had done before, would somehow make it to the Mackenzie and Fort Norman at the outlet. The decision was mine, but knowing what the *voyageurs* could do, I was confident there was no question in their minds.

The shores were grown with muskeg and tundra, a few spruce close in, the bay narrowing. We rounded a final point and there before us was a warehouse. Several men waited on the dock. The ship moved in carefully and was made fast. Canoes and packs were hoisted off, and we carried them to the bank below. The mouth looked harmless enough, low and lined with willow, no rapids in sight. We loaded, tied in the packs, and pushed off. The Indians looked on apathetically, said nothing. This was our affair.

We waved and were gone, rocks slipping away beneath us. They were smooth and shining, the colors of the shield from which they came, brown and gray, red and black, all of a size. The glacial moraine through which the river had cut its channel was sand, water-washed gravel, and boulders, with no ledges or outcrops to stem the flow, a smooth course with an even descent.

So absorbed was I in studying the bottom through the clear water, I almost forgot our speed, but when individual rocks began to blur, I knew we were moving fast. Small riffles showed ahead, piles of rounded boulders in midstream, but the river was wide with room to maneuver and we sped by the spouts without danger. I began to feel good again, and already Eldorado and the *Radium Gilbert* seemed like a dream. Mile after mile swept behind us, miles of speed and constant movement. We could see white horses far ahead, but knowing the character of the river bed, their running was sheer delight. Occasionally there were clusters of them where boulders had been piled helter-skelter by the ice and high waters of the breakup, but always in between or on either side were gleaming, unbroken slicks.

"So this," I thought, "was the river we must not run."

My bowman, Tyler Thompson, was one of the best I've ever known. At the start he watched the river narrowly, his paddle poised for any emergency, but after a while when he saw what the river was like, he relaxed.

"Bourgeois," he said happily, "I find I must rest," and with that he put his feet up on the bow, slid off his seat onto a pack behind him, fixed a pillow with his old red sweater and settled down.

"Tyler, my friend," I replied, "the fleshpots of Eldorado were too much for an aging *voyageur*. Your conduct is unbecoming."

"Ah, *oui*," he said sadly, snuggling down still further, "it comes to all men, but I am glad we were there."

As we swept around the wide curves, all I had to do was steer. This was different from any river we had ever run, no sudden gorges or ledges, no complete blocking of the channel, a smooth ride down for all the world like a long, well-graded chute. Toward late afternoon, after some thirty-five miles, we landed above the famed and fearsome rapids of the Charles, were swept into the bank so fast I was forced to make a swift turn with the bow upstream.

"Bourgeois," Tyler admonished me, "you disturbed my sleep."

We carried the canoes up on the rocks, covered our packs, and spent the night with the portage crew who unloaded barges and transported freight by truck around the rapids. Again bunks, warm meals, and once more the warnings.

"Better not run the Charles," they said, "the rest of the river maybe, but certainly not Charles Rapids."

One Indian, a packer for the outfit, told of running afoul a rock halfway through, and standing in icy water up to his neck for an hour before he got his canoe off the ledge.

He smiled when I said we would make the run in the morning and I knew what he was thinking. We were there bright and early, the sun shining, the river enticing as the day before. It was inconceivable its character could change—the broad sweeping curves, the glistening spouts in the distance, the sensation of speed—but even so we were alert because of the warnings.

The river narrowed, became even swifter, and in places billows began to roll. Ahead loomed ramparts with massive abutments crowding close. Thicker and thicker grew the spouts, most of them caused by boulders, but some I knew by ledges of native rock. Tyler leaned forward watching, his paddle sweeping warily over the surface, digging in to avoid something close, poised like a spear to shift us to either side.

The first few miles went well, always Vs between the white horses or near the banks, no raging billows we could not ride with ease. Tyler was in his element, riding our canoe as though he were skiing down a slope with the snow exactly right. What a joy to watch him and support his every move with power from my own paddle. Then white water showed all over the channel, for just ahead a mountain came down to the valley. Black, broken rocks were showing now with boulders everywhere, spray shooting high above them. Somewhere between must be a way; such speed and volume could not be contained. Far to the right was a channel and we shot across at a sharp angle to the current, slipped into the channel, and were hurtling down faster than we had ever gone.

Then it was over, the river sweeping on as before, the shouting and tumult behind us. Tyler rested on his paddle, turned, and looked back up the river.

"We made it," he said, grinning, "but barely. Let's go ashore and stretch our legs."

The canoes landed on a broad bank of gravel where a little creek came out, and to celebrate we cooked a pot of tea. Mount Charles, for which the rapids had been named, loomed behind us. From its heights we might see the whole country, possibly even the ranges to the west.

"Let's climb it," I said, "we need to get our feet on the ground after running that river." Everyone agreed and after several hours we were high enough to see the blue gash of the Bear and its confluence with the Mackenzie, the lower rugged expanse of the course we had run in less than ten hours of actual travel time. But the most thrilling sight of all, was the snow-capped peaks of the Mackenzie mountains to the west, a northerly extension of the Rockies. Never before had we seen them from such a vantage point, never with the continental sweep that was ours after thousands of miles of travel by canoe.

One can see mountains from the air, through a train window, from a ship, or from an automobile rolling along a smooth highway, but when you see them as we did, they are entirely different. I knew as we stood there on the topmost pinnacle what Lewis and Clark meant when they said, "We see the Shining Mountains." We, too, were seeing our Shining Mountains as the explorers did, and never again would they be the same. We saw them as all men should see mountains once in their lives, from the ground, after many miles of primitive travel.

After our return to the canoes, we paddled down the rest of the Bear, shot a few final riffles, then entered the mighty flow of the wide Mackenzie, its high ice-scoured banks, its blue gentians and daisies on muddy flats, its tremendous sweep toward the ramparts and the sea. Fort Norman was upstream barely a mile, so up we went to pay our respects. The Hudson's Bay Company manager invited us to his home, and within half an hour his immaculate living room was crowded with people, the nurse, the school teacher, a missionary, the Mounted Police, wives and friends, and many others. We had tea in delicate china cups, and freshly baked cakes, talked about our trip and the world outside. They were hungry to talk, but perhaps more hungry to see new faces, urged us to stay the night, have a dance, a real party, but we told them sadly we must push on to Norman Wells. We sat and talked for several hours, felt hot and closed-in and somewhat ill at ease in our bush clothes, while through the window we could see the broad Mackenzie rolling by.

An Indian Chief made a speech and presented us with a small replica of a skin boat. I, too, made a speech, accepting the gift for all the *voyageurs* of the expedition, and told him that whenever we looked at it, we would remember the occasion of our visit to Fort Norman and the friendship all had shown. When it was time to go, everyone came down to see us off.

As we stood there at the landing, the Indian pointed to Bear Rock, told how a giant hunter once lived there, killed beaver in the valley and dragged the bloody carcasses up over the cliffs.

"Look," he said, "you can see the blood."

I looked and there was the hunter's trail still red with the blood of his beaver.

"A Great Hunter," said the Chief, "gone long time now, long time ago, but his mark still there."

We pushed off into the channel, waved good-by once more and headed north for Norman Wells. To our right for over a

229

mile was Bear Rock, and the blood shone in the light of the sun.

Good-by to the Great Hunter of the past, and to Fort Norman, Fort Franklin, to Great Bear, Eldorado, and Conjuror Bay. Good-by to all the north with its legends, its high sounding valiant names, to romance, distance, and aloneness.

CHAPTER 19

SPELL OF THE YUKON

I DID NOT reach the Yukon until a few years ago, but long before that my vision of it was a vivid one, painted by that master of far-north balladry, Robert Service. Somehow in spite of grandiloquent language, a highly romantic interpretation of the land of the famous gold strike of ninety-eight, his ballads caught something nebulous that no one else quite achieved, a quality that even today over half a century later enthralls those who know the bush and the life of the frontiers.

Ever since that memorable day of my boyhood when I discovered him, the Yukon meant something special to me.

The very sound of the name had magic, a land of wild, primitive beauty where men made fortunes in gold or lost all they had, where they struggled and died against impossible odds. Born too late to take part in the great adventure, I was thrilled by the tales that came out of those fabulous years. Though I had talked to men who had been there, fondled their nuggets, listened in awe and envy as they told what they had done, it was Robert Service who made the Yukon come alive for me; and I can quote him yet with as much feeling as when I first ran across his booklet of gold-rush ballads.

> *There's a whisper on the night wind, there's a*
> *star agleam to guide us,*
> *And the wild is calling, calling . . . let us go.*

There was the essence of my feeling for the Yukon. I lived with the words "And the wild is calling, calling—let us go" until the far reaches of the north became an obsession with me and at times I was filled with unbearable longing for a land I had never known. When I could stand it no longer, I often took my dog-eared volume and read aloud the lines that gripped me most.

> *Have you gazed on naked grandeur where there's*
> *nothing else to gaze on?*
> *In the hush of mountained fastness, in the flush*
> *of midnight skies.*
> *I am the land that listens, I am the land that broods.*

The pictures those words painted of the Yukon stayed with me. Though I have seen much wild country in my roamings since those early impressionable years, because of Service, the Yukon stood apart and alone and for me assumed the stature of a haunting legend. Several times in my travels I came close to its borders and once even glimpsed its shining peaks from the Mackenzie River's Mount Charles, below Fort Norman. As I sat there that day, high above the valley and looked off to the west, the old thrill was still there and I knew before long I must make my sentimental journey to the fields of gold and romance.

When I finally did reach the Yukon, I had seen too much to expect it to be the land I had imagined. I knew however, that somewhere away from roads and towns, and airplanes, I would find what Service had written about. My expedition would in a sense be a search for a long lost boyhood dream.

I landed at historic Skagway, once the roughest and most notorious camp in the world, the port which was the jumping-off place for the gold rush. Here was where the ships put in, coming north from Seattle and San Francisco. Skagway had actually changed little, the vistas of glistening ice fields, the towering mountains seen from the Lynn Canal were the same, the beach and the flat where once thousands of tents were pitched, with equipment and supplies strewn helter-skelter from end to end, the main street with its false-fronted buildings, the terrible trail itself leading from the flat and winding up through the pass. I walked up and down

Broadway and imagined how it had been in 1898, but somehow it seemed unreal, a sort of movie backdrop with a worn-out facade of the past.

True, this is where it all began and I could see the route going up through the gorge, the desperate forty-five miles that had tried men's souls. I did not make the climb as they did, but rode over it on a narrow-gauge railway, the White Pass and Yukon, built to transport men and supplies to the head of navigation above the Yukon River.

In places, from the train windows, the trail could still be seen and I pictured the long line of men packing their outfits up that killing slope in waist deep snow, sensed their desperate hurry and confusion. As the train clattered on. I remembered the beaten and starving mules and horses, the stench of rotting flesh in Dead Horse Gulch—once filled with so many carcasses, the trail led over them. But recapturing the scene from a comfortable seat on a train was impossible. That was another age, and the lines of Service seemed without meaning or authenticity.

> *Never was seen such an army, pitiful, futile, unfit,*
> *Never was seen such a spirit, manifold courage and grit.*

When the train climbed up over the divide, I stood on the platform and felt the icy winds sweeping across the smooth glaciated surfaces of the plateau. Many, I knew, had turned back there rather than continue to the water of Lake Bennett.

Before me was the bay where ten thousand men once camped while building boats and scows for their trip down the river to the gold fields. An old weather-beaten church still stood; on top of the rise a few tumble-down cabins were scattered along the slope; beyond was nothing but brush and scrubby trees, clear across the valley.

"Isn't it exciting," said someone beside me, "just imagine what took place here."

I looked at a faded photograph of the sea of tents, the black clots of men, but somehow it still seemed unreal.

I am the land that listens, I am the land that broods.

We stopped for lunch at Bennett. It was served mining camp style on long tables to give the atmosphere of the days of ninety-eight. The food was good and plentiful, but I was glad when we moved on. This was interesting and I enjoyed seeing the old places I had read about, but nowhere yet was the feeling of that elusive something I had come to find.

At White Horse that night, a bustling frontier town with dusty streets, grinding trucks, a thirteen-million-dollar airport, and a sort of bursting-at-the-seams vitality, I found a quiet eating place down near the old Yukon River waterfront. The restaurant dated back proudly to the good old days and had not changed much in sixty years. The walls were covered with pictures, maps and mementos. Not far away was the landing, and after dinner I walked over there to look at the Yukon steamers now up on dry land, the remnants of a fleet of once-proud river boats, scroll work on their bridges and, along their sides, tall stacks and enormous paddle wheels. They were the type that plied the Mississippi long after the Civil War, the *Showboat*, the *Robert E. Lee*, the *Henry Clay*. These had different names, *Klondike*, *Dawson City*, *Casca*, *Tagish*, but were much the same—wood burners made to navigate a river with sand bars, rapids, and sharp bends. Now they sat waiting to be dismantled. Only one would be kept as a museum and for an occasional trip down river. It was now being rebuilt, smoke was coming out of its stacks, and on shore a pile of cordwood waited to be loaded.

As I stood there, I thought of the thousands who had ridden those boats to Dawson City at the mouth of the Klondike, men full of dreams and hopes, how some had stayed while others returned, broken and lost, or with fortunes that stirred uncounted others to come and try their luck. I thought of the heartbreak, suffering, and starvation of these men who, unprepared—and many just off city streets—had suddenly come face to face with an untamed, rugged land, with brutality, hunger and greed, of the frenzy with which they streamed from the gold hungry states to the frozen north with the cry: "Gold—Gold in the Klondike—On to the Yukon," until it seemed as though they had been seized with madness.

Still I felt there must be something more that drove many

of them on, something more impelling than the lure of the gold itself or the chance of making a fortune—the fierce wild beauty of the land and the test in pitting their strength against it, the comradeship in sharing hardship, disaster, and triumph, the vast and utter loneliness, the joyous song of a creek tumbling down a mountain side, the feel of spring after the stark and bitter cold of a long winter. This was the backdrop to the search for gold and when Service wrote: "Men of the High North, the wild sky is blazing," he was thinking of all this, and deep down in his heart, in all the strange tales he wove into his ballads, was the feeling of men for the north.

The following morning I went over to Miles Canyon above White Horse. A dam had been built at the foot of the rapids, so it was no longer the raging flood it had been. I studied the river where so many had come to grief, where food, supplies, and equipment that had been packed over the White Pass was lost forever. From the rocky banks of the gorge, I tried to see it as it used to be, the surge of white horses and the high crest in the center, the treacherous cliffs and rocks on either side and at its base. As a canoeman with many rapids behind me, I could understand why that stretch of river had thrown fear into all and why lives had been lost there.

It was while standing below Miles Canyon that I first began to get an intimation of the feeling I had been searching for. Picturing the old swirls and danger spots described so vividly in the diaries, it seemed I could see above me the waiting men who, having battled their way over the trail, were now ready to make the last supreme effort to reach their goal. To these Cheechakos, the name given to tenderfeet, it was a matter of life and death. This rapids would settle the score.

Shooting the wrath of my rapids, scaling my ramparts of snow.

Service had caught it all, the fear of men hurtling down that wild canyon in boats and scows, men who knew nothing of white water, I could see the ungainly craft yaw and swing in the cross currents and whirlpools, then crack up against the rocks. Forgotten at the moment was the train ride up and over the pass from Skagway, the lunch at Lake Bennett, the remains of old mining camps. This seemed real at last.

But it was not until I made a trip into the country south and west of the Yukon with my son Sig and with Joe Langevin, a game warden, that I came to the end of my quest. We were in the Kluane Game Sanctuary and had climbed to a broad and open plateau.

"Here," said Joe, "is sheep country, we'll sit here a while and look over the skyline."

Around us were snow-covered ranges and peaks. We were in a great amphitheater and had grandstand seats. The warden had a spotting scope and field glasses and was studying the ridges intently.

"There they are," he said finally, "about thirty."

He handed me the glasses and I saw them at once, a cluster of white dots against the brown tundra-covered hillsides. But through the spotting scope those little dots became ewes and rams, almost, it seemed, within a stone's throw. They were feeding and resting undisturbed for we were too far away for them to hear us or get our scent. One great ram stood on an outcrop away from the rest. He did not feed, simply stood there and watched.

"Dall sheep," said Joe, "this is one of the best places for them in the whole Yukon."

Within a couple of hours we had spotted 191 sheep in small, scattered groups on the slopes around us. Some were near, within half a mile, but most were at least twice that far.

I left my companions after a time and walked toward one of the groups, crossed a low ridge, and was alone. It was as though I had walked through an open door and closed it quietly behind me. Then I became aware of the immensity of the scene and the silence. Below lay a bank of ice and snow, brown and discolored for the wind had blown its dust upon it. A ground squirrel chittered at me from its burrow to one side. Small brown birds that looked like siskins twittered and flew around the ice, feeding on the seeds of grasses and flowers which had bloomed there a month before. The twittering in that all engulfing quiet was almost loud. Never before had those tiny flute-like notes seemed so distinct and clear. The sheep paid no attention to me, worked their way up and down the hills as though I were not there.

I've stood in some mighty mouthed hollow
That's plumb full of hush to the brim.

Here was the hush; a sense of enormous and almost crushing silence lay over the land. This was the old Yukon at last.

In the afternoon we went up to Bullion Creek to see a placer operation there, crossed and crisscrossed the stream with its braided channels and shifting gravel bars, finally came to a power shovel with a drag line, a bulldozer and a sluice. A two-man operation, it was small compared to some of the great dredges working out of Fairbanks. We heard the machines long before we saw them, a yellow monster of clanking noise and steel squatting in the middle of the stream chewing its way into the gold-bearing gravel, a bulldozer pushing the dirt into a sluice which disgorged the worthless rock and kept the gold. In an hour's time, this combination could do more work than a lone prospector could do in many days. The outfit cost a great deal of money but in a good season might sluice out fifty thousand dollars worth of gold. Each time the clean-up came and the final washing was done, a small fortune was made, but the work was hard, dangerous and dirty, and the men who tended their behemoths seldom slept—for the season was short. The lure of gold and the hardship was there.

With such equipment, the whole bottom of a creek could be dug out and sluiced. Nothing was missed and, when the monsters were through, the bed of a stream looked as though it had been gouged by a glacier; only a vast and tumbled mass of moraine remained.

Ripping the guts of my mountains, looting the beds of my creeks.

The search was going on as of old, with the same desperate violence, the same struggle, but back in ninety-eight, it was more of a personal thing, man against nature with only his own strength and courage to sustain him. This was finding gold too, but it wasn't like wading into a creek, panning the gravel and sand, and seeing the color there.

So we picked up shovels and pans from one of the cabins, went down to a place where it looked as though the creek bottom had not been disturbed. I dug out a shovelful of dirt close to the bed rock, dumped it into my pan, dipped up some water and began to slosh it gently with a circular motion, washing clay and larger particles of rock out over the rim. After a time I added more water and again got rid of what I did not want. Gradually the water cleared, with only black sand remaining. This was pay dirt and I continued very carefully until there was nothing more to come out. At the end only a spoonful remained and this I held to the light.

Color! A thin flake of gold no more than an eighth of an inch in size was in the pan. It was clean and yellow and I looked at it with delight, picked it up and dropped it carefully into a small bottle. Another shovelful of dirt and I began

241

again, ending up as before, with a tiny residue. Beside the sand were several small grains, miniature nuggets exactly like the big ones, except for size. Those yellow grains of gold were what led men up the little nameless creeks, watching, always watching for color as they searched and panned every likely looking prospect.

"A hard working miner could make a grubstake here," said Joe, "and possibly a little more beside."

We kept on and were oblivious of time. The creek gurgled merrily by and as I looked into it I saw the black ledges of volcanic rock at its base. Against that rock and in its fissures and crevices were nuggets and flakes of gold settled-out over many centuries. Heavier than the other components of the stream bed, these fragments from some mother lode above had been washed out of the grand matrix in ten thousand or a million springs. The bed of the creek itself was a long sluice box, the flood waters doing the work over and over again, the gold always sinking to the bottom. It was simply dredging on a gigantic scale.

I left my panning finally and turned over a few boulders, examining them carefully underneath. Where they had lain against the clay might be a few flakes or even a nugget or two if the boulder had not been moved. Though I searched carefully, I found nothing.

"All this stuff must have come from upstream," said Sig, as he carefully screened the last sand from his panning, "this didn't just happen."

Joe laughed, "That's what always got 'em," he said, "any man who has ever seen color in his pan has looked upstream and wondered."

I knew the prospectors had swarmed over every tributary of the Yukon and the Klondike for hundreds of miles in all directions from Dawson City at its mouth. Not a chance had been overlooked in the frantic quest. They left their diggings almost before they began, worked upstream—staking out claims as they went—in the hope of finding the mother lode and a bonanza. An old prospector still working a claim on the Klondike put it well.

"This country," he said, "is too big to know all of it. In the early days, they were in a hurry and couldn't possibly have covered every chance. Why," he exclaimed, and I could see the old gleam in his eyes, "there's big stretches no one has ever been in."

> *For once you've panned the speckled sand and seen the*
> *bonny dust,*
> *Its peerless brightness blinds you like a spell.*
> *It's little else you care about; you go because you must,*
> *And you feel that you could follow it to hell.*

This was the Yukon men talked about, the lure of gold that brought so many thousands to the far north. In the little panning I had done, I had caught just a hint of what the old-time prospectors had known. But the part of the Yukon they seldom mentioned was the irresistible spell of a vast and lonely land, its enormous silences, its challenge, and primeval power. The land had changed, it was true, but its elusive spell was still there. Even those who returned to civilization, long after they had forgotten the gold and spent the riches they had found, remembered that while they were in the Yukon their lives had been washed with color.

"Once you've known the bush, you're never the same," is an old adage in the north. While the reason for coming was gold, it was the bush that changed men's lives. The spell of the Yukon was compounded of so many things no man could ever define it. Even Service failed, but in the line "And the Wild is calling—calling," he caught something, and all who have known the country understand what he was trying to say. He touched a responsive chord in the hearts and minds of millions of men.

CHAPTER 20

ALASKAN WILDERNESS

ALASKA holds within itself some of the finest wilderness scenery on the continent. An enormous peninsula a thousand miles from end to end, even its boundaries are dramatic: the rolling Pacific, the Bering Sea, the Arctic Ocean, and Canada's Territory of the Yukon.

The Brooks Range is a towering rampart against the north, the Aleutian and Alaskan Ranges a matching bulwark to the south, between them a complex of many other ranges, peaks, and valleys that are still relatively unknown and some unnamed. Along its rugged, beetling coasts are fiords, living glaciers, and icefields which remind one of an age that is past.

245

Down the very center of this wild northwest extension of the continent, crossing and recrossing the Arctic Circle itself, flows the Yukon, one of the earth's mightiest rivers, twisting and turning for almost two thousand miles until it disgorges its silt in a vast delta of tangled waterways.

In the warm, rainswept archipelago of the southeast are lush, rain forests along the coastal beaches, spruce, cedar, and hemlock, huge trees festooned with mosses in yellow-green. Quiet always reigns there for the cushion of moss underneath is soft and deep. In the north are tundras and muskegs matched only by the barren lands of Canada. As though this were not enough, Alaska's stormy Aleutian Islands extend in an unbroken chain almost halfway to Japan.

It is a land of big bears and moose, of walrus and seal, of whales and salmon. Caribou herds roam the tundras of their ancient range, goats and sheep climb the cliffs and slopes of its mountains, polar bears hunt the ice floes. Eskimos live along its western and northern coasts, Indians in the interior and the south. This was the pathway of migration of Asiatic tribes across the Bering Strait from Siberia.

Here is a land of immensity and contrasts seldom found in such extravagant profusion. No wonder then, that, in my search for wilderness, I found it there in a majesty and grandeur I had never known before. True, like all the north, Alaska has changed, but because of its size and remoteness there is still much of the wild as it used to be. It was in this region that I found the wilderness at its best, scenes so vivid and full of meaning they will never be forgotten.

John Hopkins Inlet of Glacier Bay in the southeast was such a place. As the little ship *Nunatak* pushed its careful way up into the fiord, bergs and floes became more numerous, blocks of ice so transparently green-blue they might have been dropped from the skies themselves. On the left a whale blew, turned over on its side, a flipper striking the water with a resounding smack. Then there were two lying side by side and whirling as though on a spit. Again and again they turned, and each time there was a silver spout as flippers crashed against the surface.

Porpoises were keeping steady pace with the ship; the floes grew denser and many had seals upon them. The mountainous shores were without life, for they had emerged from the glacier at the head of the inlet within the memory of man, their summits mirrored in the still waters. The boat seemed small and fragile as it threaded its way up the passage and through the reflections. Rivers of ice filled the valleys on either side, remnants of the dying glacier that once filled the entire bay.

We were within half a mile of the ice front. Seals were everywhere now, and unafraid, they swam close, their eyes large and luminous. Guillemots, murrelets, and scoters rested all around, while sea gulls convoyed us in. There was a constant rustling as the floes moved past. Sometimes they turned over, but as they steadied, the seals climbed back on them, slipping and sliding on the smooth, unstable surfaces.

The air was colder now, for we were close enough to the great mass of ice to feel its breath. Suddenly there was a muffled roar as a column of brown water and mud surged skyward, the sound reverberating from mountain to mountain. The column subsided, water heaved and the huge blocks moved up and down; the boat rode with them as though on a tidal wave. We watched the wave as it sped down the inlet, seals riding their cakes of ice as nonchalantly as though nothing had happened.

It was still once more and, had it not been for the uneasy whispering and movement of the water, we would not have known new bergs were being spawned. No sooner had the quiet descended, however, than we were conscious again of a soft rushing at the forefront of the glacier, a rushing punctuated by a succession of detonations as from an artillery barrage. Again the sense of movement, the column of spray, mud, and water, then in slow motion a huge block of ice broke away and sank into the sea.

The scene has never left me. Because of this living remnant of the past, I had returned to the glacial age at a time when with the recession of the ice, such spawnings took place all over the north. I had spanned ten thousand years of continental history in the short space of a day, had lived along the edge of the great glacier and watched its retreat.

The McNeil is a typical Alaskan river with a sand bar and a broad alluvial flat where it enters the sea. As we approached, we saw its mouth was very much alive. Salmon were running, the rapids full of them heading upstream to spawn. Brown bears were feeding, hooking the fish with their claws, grasping them with their teeth, wading in the shallows and over the rocks, gorging on the harvest as they have for uncounted centuries. One enormous old bear sat half-submerged in the water and caught the salmon as they ran against him. A bite or two and he would catch another without moving, the bloody carcasses floating downstream. This bear was great and fat; he had learned the secret of taking fish the easy way without pursuit. Leaner, hungrier bears wallowed around the slippery boulders, rushed frantically into pools, cornered their prey between the rocks or against the ledges. We counted many that morning, the far-famed brownies of Alaska.

Back of the bears were eagles, feeding on half-eaten salmon washed up on the bank. There was a constant screaming and movement of wings as the big birds hovered over their feast. Flocks of sea gulls completed the picture, and over all was the silver canopy of wings and the sound of their incessant mewing. The scene was the same when the Russians established colonies along the coast almost two centuries ago, an ecological balance not yet disturbed by man.

As I watched, it was not hard to imagine a primitive man crouched behind one of those boulders waiting to move in and get his share. Knowing a spear was no protection, he would bide his time and wait for the fish that would be his when the animals, their hunger appeased, left for the dense alder brush on either side of the river. Then like the eagles and the gulls, he would run in and scavenge with them. Carcasses lay everywhere, but still he dared not move. He was hungry, had waited long, and watched with envy. A fish drifted close and tempted, he grasped his spear, grew cautious, settled down once more.

That summer one of the dormant volcanoes in the Valley of Ten Thousand Smokes exploded, spewing smoke, gases, and ash some thirty thousand feet into the air over an area of fifty square miles, blotting out the sun in some places a hundred miles away. Shortly afterward, I flew into the region, our little plane following a valley that led toward the volcano. As we approached the interior, I was conscious of a yellowish cloud different from fog or ordinary dust. Thicker and thicker grew the haze. There was a smell of sulphur in the air and visibility dropped until it was difficult to judge altitude or direction.

I looked down and below was a bed of cinders and ash. Not a tree, a bush, or any living thing was there. Smoke and gas issued from fumeroles, evidence that volcanic forces were still alive. This, I thought, was how the earth looked several billions of years ago before its crust had cooled enough for waters to form, a span devoid of life until at last the rains formed pools and lakes and seas, and in their warm and stagnant backwaters, molecules combined to form the first organic structures.

Here was the primeval from which all life had come, including man. From such smoke and ash, molten lava and gas, had come the miracle of a creature who could turn back time, destroy all life and perhaps the planet itself. Out of that had emerged our culture, our consciousness of beauty, and a wisdom garnered over the ages which could keep the flame of spirit alive if only it willed. This was an elemental world: the expanding universe, exploding suns and meteorites, colliding nebulae, the beginning of all things and possibly their end.

Words from the Book of Revelations went through my mind:

And he opened the bottomless pit; and there smoke arose out of the pit, as the smoke of a great furnace; and the sun and the air were darkened by reason of the smoke of the. pit.

One misty day I climbed a brush-grown plateau to a look-out point unparalleled even in Alaska, where unusual vistas are commonplace. A lake lay in the distance but its waters were dull; and the muskeg and tundra, with its scattered scrub spruce, dwarf birch, and willow, dripped with moisture. One might just as well have been in a protected back-country flat as far as view was concerned.

Then a miracle happened. The low-hanging mists lifted and the sun shone forth in an unclouded sky. The distant lake became a sparkling expanse of blue, and all around me for over a hundred miles was a panorama of shining, snow-capped mountains flanked by glistening ice fields and glaciers. To the north was the great arc of the Alaskan Range, to the south the Chugaches bordering the gulf, southeast in a gigantic cluster, Mounts Wrangell, Blackburn, and Sanford. But I knew Denali, the giant of them all loomed to the west and though hidden by other summits, stood there brooding and alone.

I was breathless with the scene. No words could describe the sense of immensity, of almost limitless terrain before me. Instead of one mountain peak, there were groups and clusters; instead of one glacier, major continental ice fields with uncounted tributaries alive and flowing. Here was an overwhelming beauty that dwarfed all my preconceptions.

This had the permanence of high-mountain country everywhere, a certain feeling of stability and defiance of man's efforts to change. Such a land, I felt, should stay as it is, and fulfill its highest use for mankind as a reminder of a virgin continent. Men should be able to stand on this lookout a thousand years from now and, with such vistas around them, be at peace. No room here for little thoughts; this was a place for expansiveness of the soul and cosmic perception.

The clouds were moving in again and with their constant shifting and shadows the mountain ranges seemed like floating mirages over the horizons. Within half an hour the peaks began to disappear, each one in a final flash of light. Then the mists descended over the plateau and the scene vanished, only the dripping spruce and scrubby bush remained.

In the far north lies the Brooks Range, one of the most formidable and unknown mountain expanses of the continent. We left Fort Yukon and flew low over the mouth of the Porcupine, the river that reaches so far east it almost touches the Mackenzie. Below us lay the vast flats of the Yukon River with its thousands of ponds and bogs. To the northeast were rising foothills with the Coleen and the Sheenjek rivers which we would follow. We glimpsed the distant ranges flanking the Brooks toward the east. To the west was the Chandalar country and beyond it nothing but mountains as far as the Chukchi Sea.

The foothills dropped behind us and the Sheenjek, now laded with silt, was white and turbulent as it tumbled down the slopes. We climbed steadily, hurdled a few lesser peaks, and then were over the crest of the range itself, one of such primordial savagery, it seemed utterly presumptuous to challenge its heights in a small seaplane.

Below were precipitous peaks, jagged, black, and sharp. Naked valleys and gorges lay between them. Only when flying over the Alps had I seen such stark and threatening pinnacles, but they were friendly compared to these. There, green and verdant meadows held picturesque chalets, while villages with white church spires nestled in among them, and, connecting all the valleys, were ribbons of roads and trails. Here was nothing but rock, limitless, barren reaches, and talus slopes with no signs of man or of any living thing.

To me they looked new, as though recently emerged from some gigantic cataclysm within the earth, without time enough to have been softened by erosion. Squalls and streamers of mist swirled around knife-edged cliffs, and the little plane bounced and fought its way through them toward the headwaters of the Chandalar. To the south lay the foothills and the broad valley of the Yukon, to the north, down a slope of a hundred miles, the misty fog-shrouded shores of the Arctic Ocean.

At last we caught the gleam of the river, turned and flew down it as far as Old John Lake where the Koness River leaves to find the Sheenjek, our highway going in. We landed there and looked back at the mighty rampart we had left. At that distance, it was softened and blue, not so terribly cold and unfriendly as it seemed when we were flying above it. I knew then that what I had felt up there was an illusion, that over its brown and seemingly empty stretches, flowers bloom in exotic colors, and mosses and lichens paint rocks and hillsides,

254

that birds sing and many other creatures are at home there.

All Alaska has an early morning freshness for me. While it is not young, and some of its ranges are as ancient as any on earth, I cannot help but feel when I see such mountains as the Brooks, that this is how the Appalachians, the Rockies, and the Laurentians once were. With that realization I somehow see, with greater understanding, the long road over which not only mountains, but all life has come. Such places answer a question for me that has reverberated down through the centuries:

When I consider thy heavens, the work of thy fingers, the moon and the stars, which thou has ordained; What is man that thou are mindful of him?

EPILOGUE

I should now seal my lips and bind my
tongue from the singing of verses. I should
cease my tinkling. Since a horse grows
breathless at the end of a long journey, steel
grows sleepy in cutting summer grass, water
wearies from racing around river bends, and
even fire rests after a long night's burning,
why should a runo not grow weary and rest
after a night's joy?

I have heard it said that a racing rapids does
not endlessly drop its water nor a good
singer sing until his skill is gone. Better to
leave off singing in the middle, than to wait
until one knows no more.

—Kalevala

A NOTE ON THE TYPE

THE TEXT of this book was set on the Linotype in JANSON, a recutting made direct from type cast from matrices long thought to have been made by the Dutchman Anton Janson, who was a practicing type founder in Leipzig during the years 1668-87. However, it has been conclusively demonstrated that these types are actually the work of Nicholas Kis (1650-1702), a Hungarian, who most probably learned his trade from the master Dutch type founder Dirk Voskens. The type is an excellent example of the influential and sturdy Dutch types that prevailed in England up to the time William Caslon developed his own incomparable designs from these Dutch faces.

Composed by H. Wolff, New York. Printed and bound by The Haddon Craftsmen, Inc., Scranton, Pennsylvania.

A NOTE ABOUT THE AUTHOR

SIGURD F. OLSON, is known by a generation of wilderness canoemen as the Bourgeois, as *voyageurs* of old called their trusted leaders. The author of *The Singing Wilderness, Listening Point, The Lonely Land,* and *Runes of the North* is one of our country's well-known woodsmen and naturalists. Born in Chicago in 1899, educated at the University of Wisconsin (Geology) and the University of Illinois (Plant and Animal Ecology), he was a professor and dean until he began devoting himself entirely to wilderness interpretation and its preservation. Mr. Olson is a former President of the National Parks Association, and is still a member of its Board of Trustees. He serves on the Council of the Wilderness Society and as a consultant to the Izaak Walton League of America, the President's Quetico-Superior Committee, and since 1962 the Department of the Interior. His home is in Ely, Minnesota, gateway to the canoe country.

August 1963

DATE DUE

APR 6 '82			
30 505 JOSTEN'S			